1

The Language Kit

Kit

Writing through Grammar

John Seely

Heinemann

Heinemann Educational Publishers
Halley Court, Jordan Hill, Oxford OX2 8EJ
A division of Reed Educational and Professional Publishing Ltd

OXFORD MELBOURNE AUCKLAND
JOHANNESBURG BLANTYRE GABORONE
IBADAN PORTSMOUTH NH (USA) CHICAGO

02 01 00 99 98
10 9 8 7 6 5 4 3 2 1

ISBN 0 435 10198 6

Designed and produced by Ken Vail Graphic Design
Cover design by I E Design
Cover illustration by Anthony Rule
Illustrated by Graham-Cameron Illustration (Michelle Ives
and Brian Lee), Elizabeth Roy Literary Agency (Mike Phillips)
and Anthony Rule.
Printed and bound in Spain by Edelvive

A message for teachers

The Language Kit contains teaching materials that help you to teach grammatical concepts and to guide pupils in using this understanding of grammar in their reading and writing. Since grammar is a system it has to be introduced systematically. This means that the book is progressive; each unit assumes that the material in earlier units has been fully understood.

There are fifteen units, of which twelve are teaching units and three – numbers 5, 10 and 15 – are revision units. Each unit has ten pages.

The teaching units are based on the adventures of a female android called **LISA**. She has come to earth to learn about English and arrived at a school. This device is used to enable pupils to reflect upon and articulate their existing knowledge of English.

Each of the teaching units follows a similar pattern:

A: Introductory page
The first page contains a large picture illustrating some aspect of **LISA's** exploration of earth, followed by a small number of discussion points to get the class talking about the chosen situation. There is also a summary of the language content of the unit.

B: Language awareness
The first spread focuses on some aspect of language usage and invites pupils to reflect upon and discuss it in a structured way.

C: Grammar study
The next spread introduces and teaches the grammatical material of the unit.

D: Grammar and sentences
This spread gives pupils a chance to practise the grammar they have just learned, by completing sentences and/or writing their own.

E: Drafting and writing
The final spread contains a structured approach to writing in a particular mode or format. This is usually linked to both the language awareness and grammatical content of the unit.

F: Final page
This contains a summary of the main language points covered.

On each spread the material is progressively more demanding. Usually on the language awareness, grammar study and grammar and sentences pages, the essential material is covered on the left-hand page, while the right-hand page contains important extension material. So all pupils can work on the left-hand page material and the more able can cover both pages. The Teacher's Book indicates when this pattern is not followed.

The revision units can be used as informal tests for individual work, or for reinforcement work with the class as a whole. There are additional tests in the Teacher's Book. These can be photocopied as required.

If you have any comments on these materials and suggestions for their improvement, I should be most grateful to hear from you, via the publisher.

Contents

Through the eyes of an android

Androids are machines built to look and behave like human beings. Instead of a heart and a brain they have a computer.

A group of these creatures has been sent from Planet K48Z46 to investigate our life and language. **LISA** is the Language Investigation Specialist Android. She has got the job of learning English so that she can teach it to scientists on K48Z46.

In this unit you will learn about:

Clues about conversations

Different kinds of sentence:
- statements
- questions
- directives.

Asking questions ...
... and the different kinds of question we can ask.

Using directives ...
... and the different reasons we have for using them.

Doing an interview and writing a script

Writing instructions

Helping LISA

Exercise A

LISA has got excellent hearing and very good sight (even in the dark!). She is also very good at working out patterns. Even so, at first she can't make any sense at all of what she sees and hears in the busy street.

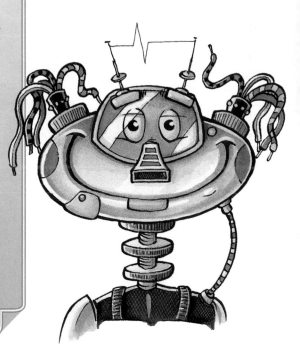

1 Think:
   a What sights and sounds do you think she would notice first?
   b What do you think the people in the street would make of her?

2 Write a list of your answers to each of the questions.

3 Talk to the rest of your group about what you think.

Exercise B

If **LISA** is going to survive on the dangerous streets of this strange planet, she needs help. She has to communicate with earth people – fast.

You can help her, by teaching her the words and sentences she needs to survive.

1 Think:
   a What do you think would be the ten most important English words that **LISA** should learn first?
   b What would be the five most important sentences she should learn to say?

2 Write down your answers to each of the questions.

3 Talk to the rest of your group about what you think.

Listening in

When you start trying to learn a foreign language, everybody seems to speak so fast. Your brain just can't keep up with all the new words and sentences you are hearing. **LISA's** on-board computer has just the same problem.

LISA can cope with the first few sentences of a conversation and then she loses it. On this page there are printouts of the beginnings of some conversations she heard on her first day on earth. Let's see if you can help **LISA** work out what is going on.

Conversation A

A: I want some crisps.
B: Put that down!
A: No.
B: Put it down or I'll ...

Conversation B

A: I'm afraid you can't stop here, madam.
B: Why can't I?
A: There's a double yellow line.
B: I only want to ...

Conversation C

A: Freshly baked today, girls. Straight out of the ovens. Brown or white, soft or crusty ... Yes dear, what would you like?
B: Half a dozen cobs, please.
A: Anything else?

Exercise A

For each of the conversations, follow these steps:

1 Read the words carefully.

2 Try to hear the conversation in your head.

3 Look at the questions below and answer each one as fully as you can.

What?		**Where?**		**Who?**
1 What are they talking about?	**3**	Where does this conversation take place?	**5**	Who is **A**?
			6	Who is **B**?
2 Are there any special words that tell you this?	**4**	What makes you think so?	**7**	How can you tell?

Different kinds of sentence

In English there are three main kinds of sentence:

Statements

If you want to **tell** someone something, you use a statement sentence:

It's pouring with rain.

Questions

If you want to **ask** someone something – to find something out – you use a question sentence:

Is it going to rain today?

Directives

If you want to **order** someone to do something, you use a directive sentence. These are also called *commands*:

Wipe your feet!

Exercise A

Look at these short conversations and find:

1 a statement sentence

2 a question sentence

3 a directive sentence.

Conversation A

A: I want some crisps.

B: Put that down!

A: No.

B: Put it down or I'll ...

Conversation B

A: I'm afraid you can't stop here, madam.

B: Why can't I?

A: There's a double yellow line.

B: I only want to ...

Exercise B

Now it's your turn to write a conversation:

- Make up a completely new conversation between two people, or
- finish one of the conversations in Exercise A.

In your conversation:

1 Start every sentence on a new line.

2 After each sentence, say if it is a statement (**S**), a question (**Q**) or a directive (**D**). Follow the example below.

> **A:** What are you doing with my new CD? (Q)
>
> **B:** I'm only looking at it. (S)
>
> **A:** Put it down! (D)

Questions and directives

LISA is having some difficulties sorting out question sentences and directive sentences. She wants you to explain them to her computer.

Questions

LISA has collected the sample sentences in Exercise A. She wants to sort them into groups. She has worked out that this sentence:

This is your pencil.

can be turned into two different questions:

A *Is this your pencil?*
B *Where is your pencil?*

LISA says: 'What is the difference between these two kinds of question?'

Directives

LISA has been told that another name for directive sentences is 'commands'. She finds that a bit puzzling. A command is when you **order** someone to do something. She has collected a number of directive sentences and they don't all sound like orders.

Exercise B

Have a look at the sentences in the box below and then write down the answers to these questions:

1 Are any of these 'commanding' or 'ordering' someone to do something? If so, which ones?

2 How would you describe the others? Try to think of a word that describes what the speaker is doing. A list of possible words has been given below to help you:

instructing	**threatening**
telling	**inviting**
asking	**suggesting**
begging	**advising**
warning	**pleading**

I *Come to the film with me tonight.*
J *Get out of my way!*
K *Lend me a pound.*
L *Have a nice time!*
M *Take it easy for a bit.*
N *Watch out for potholes.*
O *Put that in the corner, please.*

Exercise A

1 Which of the questions in the box below are like Question A? Write down their letters. Write down an answer to each one.

2 Which of the questions in the box are like Question B? Write down their letters. Write down an answer to each one.

3 Compare the two sets of answers. Can you answer **LISA's** question? Write down your answer.

C *Have you got my pencil?*
D *Where is my pencil?*
E *Who has got my pencil?*
F *Is this your pencil?*
G *Why are you using my pencil?*
H *Did you leave your pencil at home?*

Asking questions

Three kinds of question

There are three different kinds of question sentence:

1 Yes/no questions

These are questions that expect the answer 'yes' or 'no':

Would you like a fry-up for breakfast?

2 Either/or questions

In these questions you give the person a choice of two answers:

Would you like cereal or a fry-up for breakfast?

3 Question-word questions

When you answer these questions you have to think of your own answer:

What would you like for breakfast?

Half an interview

In this conversation we've only got the answers. Read it through and try to work out what the interviewer said.

INTERVIEWER:	—— Question 1 —— ?
PETER:	*Peter Knowlesley.*
INTERVIEWER:	—— Question 2 —— ?
PETER:	*I'm a deep sea diver.*
INTERVIEWER:	—— Question 3 —— ?
PETER:	*For five years.*
INTERVIEWER:	—— Question 4 —— ?
PETER:	*Yes.*
INTERVIEWER:	—— Question 5 —— ?
PETER:	*I've always liked swimming, especially in the sea. Then I had a holiday in Cornwall and had the chance to try it out.*

INTERVIEWER:	—— Question 6 —— ?
PETER:	*No, not really.*
INTERVIEWER:	—— Question 7 —— ?
PETER:	*The equipment costs quite a bit. Once you've got that, it isn't too expensive.*
INTERVIEWER:	—— Question 8 —— ?
PETER:	*Yes. Definitely.*
INTERVIEWER:	—— Question 9 —— ?
PETER:	*I've been to the Greek Islands and that's excellent. The place I'd really like to dive is the Great Barrier Reef in Australia.*
INTERVIEWER:	—— Question 10 —— ?
PETER:	*No, I haven't.*

Exercise A

What were the questions?

1 There were ten questions altogether. Write down the numbers and the questions you think the interviewer might have asked.

2 For each question you have written, write down whether it was:

A Yes/no   **B** Either/or

C Question-word.

Using directives

Directive sentences

Directive sentences are not just used to order or command someone to do something. They have many other uses. These include:

1 To invite
   Come to the film with me tonight.

2 To order
   Get out of my way!

3 To beg or plead
   Lend me a pound.

4 To wish someone well
   Have a nice time!

5 To advise
   Take it easy for a bit.

6 To warn
   Watch out for the potholes.

7 To ask or request
   Put that in the corner, please.

When you use directive sentences it is quite easy to offend, upset or amuse people. You need to think carefully about:

Who?
- Who is the person I am speaking to?
- How should this affect the way I speak or write?

Why?
- Why am I talking or writing to this person?
- What effect do I want to have on them?

Exercise A
LISA has collected some sentences and would like to know when she could use them. Look at the *Sentences* and choose the correct *Who?* from the box below this.

Sentences
1 *Walk on the right of the corridor!*
2 *Mind your head!*
3 *Give me my pencil back.*
4 *Have a good time in Blackpool!*
5 *Give me a dozen of those rolls.*

Who?
A *Parent to young child.*
B *One pupil in class to another.*
C *Teacher to pupil.*
D *Traffic warden to driver.*
E *Doctor to patient.*
F *Owner to dog.*
G *One friend to another.*
H *Boss to worker.*
I *Customer to shop assistant.*
J *One person in the street to another.*

Exercise B
There are a number of answers left in the *Who?* box. Make up an example sentence for each of them.

The interview

You have won a competition in which the first prize is to conduct a TV interview with anyone you like. It could be:

- a famous sports personality
- a film star
- a musician
- a politician
- a TV star.

1 You choose!

Think carefully about who you will interview – think of a person who will have plenty to say for themselves. When you have chosen, write the person's name at the top of the page.

2 Thinking about questions

Before the interview you need a list of questions that you will ask. Remember that it is best to ask question-word questions. These are questions that begin with the words:

Who? What? Where? How? Why? When? Which?

Think of ten good questions and write them down.

3 The interview

Now it is time to have the interview. It may go well, or there may be problems. Write the script of what happens. Don't forget to ask your ten questions, but put in extra ones if you get the chance.

Writing a script

Begin with a **description** of where the speakers are. Put it in brackets and underline it.

Write the **names** of the speakers in capital letters. Put a **colon** after them.

Write the actual **words** they say.

Put **actions and other explanations** in brackets and underline them.

(An empty room in a deserted house. SAM comes in, followed by JOHN.)

SAM: We should be all right in here.
JOHN: (Anxiously) As long as no one followed us.
(JOHN looks out of the window.)
SAM: Can you see anything?

Instructions

A common use for directive sentences is in writing instructions. Writing simple, clear instructions isn't easy. This will give you some practice.

1 Topic

You are going to write a set of instructions for a younger sister or brother. Begin by deciding what you are going to write about. Choose something that you can do well, but which your brother or sister cannot. For example:

- programming the video
- playing a computer game
- making beans on toast
- using a calculator to add up.

Write down what you have chosen.

2 Equipment

Make a list of any equipment needed.

3 Words

You may have to use a number of special words. Make a list of them and against each one write an explanation so that the reader will know what you are talking about. For example:

Channel selector switches: These are the two little buttons on the right-hand end. One has an arrow pointing up and the other one has an arrow pointing down.

4 Listing the steps

Now think carefully about *all* the actions you have to do. Make a list of them in order. When you have finished, check them carefully – it is easy to miss out an important step. (You could get someone else to help you by checking your list.)

5 Writing the instructions

Now write the instructions out in full, using the notes you have made.

Summing up what you've learned

Important questions

When we write something we need to ask these questions:

What?
Exactly what am I writing about?

Who?
Who am I writing this for?

Why?
What effect do I want to have on them?

Where?
Where am I doing this piece of writing? Is it a letter, a set of notes for school, or what?

Three kinds of sentence

In English there are three main kinds of sentence:

Statement
A statement tells the reader something:
> *It's pouring with rain.*

Question
A question sentence asks for information:
> *Is it going to rain today?*

Directive
A directive sentence tells someone to do something:
> *Wipe your feet!*

More about questions

There are three kinds of question:

1 **Yes/no questions:**
   Would you like a fry-up for breakfast?

2 **Either/or questions:**
   Would you like cereal or a fry-up for breakfast?

These questions must contain the word 'or'.

3 **Question-word questions:**
   What would you like for breakfast?

These questions start with one of these words:

who	whom	whose	what
where	why	when	how
which			

More about directives

Directive sentences are used for several different purposes. The commonest are:

1 **To invite**
   Come to the film with me tonight.

2 **To order or command**
   Get out of my way!

3 **To beg or plead**
   Lend me a pound.

4 **To wish someone well**
   Have a nice time!

5 **To advise**
   Take it easy for a bit.

6 **To warn**
   Watch out for the potholes.

7 **To ask or request**
   Put that in the corner, please.

LISA goes to school

This is **LISA's** first day at school. You can probably remember your first day at your present school quite clearly.

- What were your most important thoughts and feelings before you left home?
- What were your thoughts and feelings as you arrived at the school for the first time?
- What did you find most difficult or confusing that first day?
- What was the best thing that happened to you?

Some schools give new pupils a very careful introduction to their new school. What do you think is the best way to prepare new pupils?

If you were given the responsibility of introducing **LISA** to her new school, how would you set about it?

In this unit you will learn about:

The language of school ...
... who says **what** to **whom** and where and **why**.

Making a dictionary

Word classes:
- nouns
- personal pronouns.

Parts of a sentence:
- the subject.

Writing:
- how to **plan** and **draft** a description of your first day at a new school.

LISA goes to school

On her first day at school, **LISA** thinks her computer will blow up! It's got so many new words to process, it just can't cope. Schools seem to have a language that is all their own.

School messages

1 Where's your homework?

2 Write this in your exercise books.

3 Don't you know your nine times table yet?

4 Pupils must not run in the corridors.

5 Lower School Reception.

6 India became independent in 1947.

LISA needs someone to explain what all these strange messages mean. The more information you can give her about each one the better. Remember: she has never been inside a school before and knows nothing about lots of things you take for granted.

Exercise A

LISA likes things set out neatly. Explain the messages by copying and completing this table:

No.	Who?	What? And where?	Why?
1	A teacher to a pupil.	In a classroom. The teacher is asking about work the pupil should have done at home.	The teacher wants to see the homework.
2			
3			

Making a dictionary

Life would be a lot easier for **LISA** if she had a list of all the words she needed for school with explanations of what they meant – a sort of school dictionary. Perhaps you can help her.

Exercise A

1 Make a list of all the words **LISA** is likely to need.
Think of words for:
- places in school
- school subjects
- school occasions (like 'assembly')
- people at school (like 'headteacher')
- things you need at school (like 'pencil case').

2 Go through your list and choose five words for your dictionary.

3 Write a dictionary definition of each one.

An example has been given to help you.

> **school**
> 1 a place where children or young people go to learn (e.g. 'primary school', 'high school')
> 2 a large group of fish (e.g. 'a school of cod').

Exercise B

About a hundred years ago Ambrose Bierce, an American journalist, wrote a different kind of dictionary. Instead of giving straight explanations of what words meant, he told readers what he thought of the things he was writing about. For example:

> **circus:** A place where horses, ponies and elephants are permitted to see men, women and children acting the fool.

You could do the same thing for your school dictionary. For example, how would you define 'school'?

1 Make a list of five school words to write about.

2 For each one write a joke dictionary definition.

LISA's job today is to find out about nouns and pronouns. The school has helped her. It has given her a page from its guide for new pupils. **All the nouns are printed in blue, like this.** *And all the pronouns are printed in pink, like this.*

What to do

LISA wants you to explain to her:

1   What exactly is a noun?
2   What exactly is a pronoun?
3   Why do some of the nouns begin with capital letters?

Write down your answers to these questions.

Welcome to Llantarnam School. My name is Jill. I've been here a year now so there's a lot to tell you about. We have a big school but once you know where some of the places are it will seem quite small.

Exercise A

The next part of the school guide is given below. Help **LISA** find the nouns and pronouns in each sentence. It has been printed in separate sentences to make it easier. At the end of each sentence it tells you how many nouns and pronouns to look for.

1   You will be doing lots of new, exciting subjects. (2 nouns, 1 pronoun)
2   If you like sport, then you'll be pleased to know that we've got a sports complex and a gym. (4 nouns, 3 pronouns)
3   If you like music then we have a junior choir and a school orchestra. (4 nouns, 2 pronouns)
4   We also get a chance to be in the school play. (3 nouns, 1 pronoun)

Exercise B

In the next part of the guide some of the nouns and pronouns have been missed out. See if you can work out what they should be. Write down:

❶ the number of each space

❷ the word you think should go in it

❸ whether it is a noun or a pronoun.

___1___ have probably noticed lots of things that are different in your new ___2___. Perhaps the first ___3___ you saw was that this school is a lot bigger than your old ___4___. In your new school you have lots of ___5___, teaching you different subjects. By now you have probably met most of the teachers who are going to teach you in different ___6___. Maybe ___7___ have realized that no two ___8___ are the same! Let's have a look at some different ___9___ and see what ___10___ are like.

LISA investigates sentence subjects

LISA has worked out that every statement sentence has a subject.
In these sentences the subjects have been underlined in green.

> 1 Prefects help to run the school in many ways.
> 2 They have places all round the school.
> 3 They are on duty at break and lunch time.
> 4 Usually prefects are very helpful.
> 5 All the pupils in the 5th year are given the chance to become prefects.

What LISA wants to know

Write down your answers to these questions:

1 Where does the subject come in these sentences?
2 If the subject is just one word, what kind of word is it?
3 What is the subject *for*? What kind of information does it give us?

Exercise A

Write down the subjects of these sentences:

> 1 Prefects are usually very helpful.
> 2 You can recognize them from their uniform.
> 3 They wear a different tie from other pupils.
> 4 In school, you should obey the prefects' instructions.
> 5 All pupils should obey them in the bus queue, too.

Exercise B

The subjects of these sentences are missing. Write down the number of each space and the word or words that you think should go in it.

Homework

___1___ is given to help you. ___2___ is practice. ___3___ will help you to build up the homework timetable. ___4___ work out together the different subjects to go on different nights. So ___5___ get an even spread of work. ___6___ takes a little time to work out. Probably in the first few days ___7___ will ask you to do things like covering your books. ___8___ is not a good idea to work with the TV on. ___9___ just distract you. ___10___ can't work well while eating or drinking, either. ___11___ is much better to find a quiet place on your own.

Using nouns and pronouns

Exercise A

LISA has not really got the hang of personal pronouns, so she just doesn't use them when she writes. The sentences below this are what she wrote for her first school homework. Write it out again, using pronouns to make it shorter and get rid of the repetitions.

LISA went to school today. The school is very large and rather confusing. When **LISA** reached the school **LISA** was taken to the office to meet the headteacher. The headteacher told **LISA** that **LISA** was in Class 7Y. The headteacher asked Mrs Dawson to take **LISA** to **LISA's** classroom. Mrs Dawson was very busy and walked very fast, so **LISA** was left behind and got lost.

Exercise C

The five words given below were picked out of the dictionary at random. Can you make connections between them? Make up a story that connects all five. Your story must include all five nouns, but they can be in any order you like.

- tree
- feather
- toad
- dinghy
- monument

Exercise B

One of the boys in **LISA's** class has the opposite problem: he uses pronouns too often and doesn't make it clear who or what they refer to. Here is what he wrote in an English lesson about 'My favourite hobby':

David Briers is my best friend and I also go around with Ravi Gupta. He (1) lives round the corner from me. We have mountain bikes. His is red and mine is blue. It (2) has 15 speeds but the saddle isn't very comfortable. It (3) is a bit small. We like doing cross-country rides. There's a good track down by the canal and another round the back of his house. It (4) is about three miles and usually very muddy except in the summer when it dries up. It (5) doesn't matter because it is an all-weather bike.

There are five pronouns printed in pink. Each one has a number after it. Each one is not clear, because it could refer to more than one person or thing.

1. Write down the number of each pronoun.

2. For each one, explain the two people or things it could refer to.

3. Rewrite the whole text so that it is obvious what it means and no one can be confused.

Subjects and sentences

Exercise A

School has been too much for **LISA**. She wanted to write her day's report in English, but her on-board language computer malfunctioned. This is how it came out:

A	B
1 I	are full of tables and chairs.
2 It	come into these rooms and sit down.
3 Most of the rooms	is a large building with many different rooms.
4 Children	is called a lesson.
5 An adult	listen to her.
6 She	look out of the window at the rain.
7 Some of them	stands in front of them.
8 Other children	talks to them for an hour.
9 This	visited a school today.

The computer has split each of **LISA's** sentences into two parts:

A the subject
B the rest of the sentence.

All the subjects are in the right place. To help **LISA** you need to give each subject the right ending.

What to do

1 Write down the first part of Sentence 1.

2 Look in Column B and find the words that go with it.

3 Write them down to complete the sentence.

4 Now do the same for Sentence 2, and so on.

Exercise B

The subject of the sentence often gives us a very good idea of what the sentence is about. **LISA's** class are writing down their first impressions of their new school. One girl has written down all the sentence subjects but can't think how to end the sentences. The sentence subjects are listed in the box on the right. Can you help the girl out by writing the rest of each sentence?

Our new school...

The school buildings...

Most of the teachers...

English lessons...

Our English teacher...

Breaktime...

Homework...

My first impressions of school...

My friends...

First day at school: ideas

Going to a new school can be a worrying prospect. It helps if you know what is likely to happen. One way you can find out is by meeting people already at the school and hearing what they have to say about it.

Suppose *you* had to tell pupils at the local primary school what it was like coming to your new school. What would you tell them?

I was worried before I came here. I thought coming to this school from my old school but

When I first came here I thought I wouldn't b way to my lessons and I would get told off or being late but we had an excuse for being late

My first lesson was history. I was nervous know what to bring but it was fun. Then thr went from teacher to teacher having new book and form on them.

After a few days I had settled down. We were gi and were reassured that everything was going to

I have been here four months and everything have settled down in class and made new friends

Exercise A
The first thing to do is to collect your ideas together. Take five minutes and jot down as many ideas as you can. Focus on what it was like during your first day at your new school.

Starters
Here are some starter suggestions:
- feeling lost
- funny things that happened
- fears
- exciting moments
- new subjects
- teachers
- embarrassing moments
- what people said – before ... and after.

But you will have ideas of your own, too.

Exercise B
If you are lucky, you will have lots of ideas to write about. We are going to focus on just *five*.

Look through what you have written and choose the five most interesting ideas. Put a ring round the ones you choose.

Exercise C
You are going to write a short description of 'My first day at _____ School'. You have chosen five things to write about. Now decide on the *order* in which to write about them. Write them down in that order, numbered 1–5.

First day at school: writing sentences

Exercise D

1. You should now have a list of five topics, like this:
   - Arriving on the first day
   - Getting lost going to maths
   - Meeting Mrs Carson!
   - The first PE lesson
   - School dinner.

2. Begin by writing down this sentence:

   > I shall always remember my first day at _____ School.

   Write the name of your school in the blank.

3. Now look at the first topic and write four or five sentences about it. Don't worry if some of them seem very similar – or say the same thing in different ways. An example has been given below to help you.

   > I shall always remember my first day at Ramford High School. I went to school on the school bus. I went in with Paula Richards. She's my friend from primary school. We didn't know what to expect. We just stood there feeling confused.

Exercise E

4. Now look at your sentences. You are going to keep the first one. The rest of them have to be cut down to just *two*. Do it like this:
   - cross out any that aren't very good

     > I shall always remember my first day at Ramford High School. I went to school on the school bus.

   - try to find sentences that can be joined together, or tidied up.

     > I went in with Paula Richards, She's my friend from primary school.

5. When you've finished, write out your sentences again. Make sure they make good sense together.

   > I shall always remember my first day at Ramford High School. I went in with Paula Richards, my friend from primary school. We didn't know what to expect, so we just stood there feeling confused.

Exercise F

6. Now do the same with your other four topics. **Remember, for each one:**
   - Write four or five sentences.
   - Cut them down to two sentences.
   - Write the finished sentences out again.
   - Make sure that they still make sense.

This process is called **drafting**. It may seem rather slow and tiresome, but it is the best way to write really well. It is how professional writers work.

Summing up what you've learned

Nouns

We use nouns to refer to:
- people
- ideas
- things
- mixtures of all three.

Most nouns will fit into one or more of the spaces in sentences like these:

That is a(n) _____ .
There are many _____ s.
_____ is very important.

These are all nouns:
mother rope happiness town Wayne

Common and proper nouns

Nouns can be divided into two groups:
- **Proper nouns** are the names of particular people, places, books, TV programmes, films, and things like that. They are written with a capital letter at the beginning:
  John Smith
  London
  Starship Enterprise
- **Common nouns** are all the other nouns that are not proper nouns.

Sentence subjects

The subject of a statement sentence:
- comes at or near the beginning of the sentence
- usually tells us what the sentence is about
- can be one word or a group of words.

If the subject is a single word it can be:
- a noun
- a pronoun.

Pronouns

Pronouns refer back to something that has already been mentioned in a piece of writing. They can refer back to:
- a word – like a noun or another pronoun
- a group of words, a phrase
- an idea.

We use pronouns to avoid repeating things. It is important to make sure that the reader understands exactly what each pronoun refers to. There are several different types of pronoun, but some of the commonest are personal pronouns.

Personal pronouns

Personal pronouns are used instead of the names of people and things. They are:

I/me   she/her   it
we/us   he/him   they/them
you

Planning and drafting

Good writing takes a long time. You have to go through several stages:

Planning
- having ideas
- selecting the best
- putting them in the right order.

Drafting
- writing sentences
- rewriting sentences
- throwing away sentences that are no good.

What are they like?

- How would you describe what **LISA** looks like?
- What are the main things we talk about when we describe someone?
- How many different reasons can you think of for wanting a description of another person?
- What marks out a *good* description of a person from a bad one?

In this unit you will learn about:

Writing about people:
- how to describe what they look like
- how to describe their personalities.

Adjectives:
- using them with nouns
- using them to describe people
- using them in sentences.

Drafting and writing:
- planning a description of someone
- finding the words
- building the sentences.

Writing about people

Some writers have the knack of summing people up in just a few words. Read these short extracts and see what sort of picture they conjure up in your mind:

Anna Cotman
A smiling girl, with light brown hair and a round freckled face.
Vivien Alcock

The man on the beach
A paunchy man with wide hips and very short legs.
Roald Dahl

Lindy Miller
She was a teller of tales and a plotter of sly revenges. A bossy girl, quick to quarrel and slow to forgive. *Vivien Alcock*

Each of these descriptions picks out a few important details and leaves the rest to our imagination. But which details?

Describing what they look like

Face
We look first at a person's face – it often gives us clues about what they are like. Writers often take care to describe a person's face.

Clothing
Another clue to what someone is like comes from their clothing. So it's a good idea to tell the reader what the person is wearing.

The rest of the body
It is also useful to pick out any other part of the person's body that marks them off from other people.

The ratty-faced man
He was a small ratty-faced man with grey teeth. His eyes were dark and quick and clever, like a rat's eyes, and his ears were slightly pointed at the top. He had a cloth cap on his head and he was wearing a greyish-coloured jacket with enormous pockets.

I glanced at his fingers. They were so beautifully shaped, so slim and long and elegant, they didn't seem to belong to the rest of him at all.

Exercise A

1 Choose one of the people in the pictures on page 29. Look carefully at the picture.

2 Focus on the face. Make a list of words that describe what that person looks like.

3 Now imagine the rest of the person – and the clothes they are wearing. Make a list of words to describe them.

3 Choose a second person and do the same for them.

Describing their personality

The other main way in which you can describe people is to say
what they are like 'inside'.

Summing them up
The most important
thing to do is to choose
words that sum up
what the person is like.
The key word here is
'frivolous'. It means
'silly or light-hearted,
rather than serious and
sensible'. Writers often
select several words
that sum a person up.

Hazel Brent is my best
friend… She is always laughing.
To be honest, she is rather
frivolous. That's why I like her so
much. She's fun to be with.

If I told Hazel about my
problem, she would shriek and
giggle and tell the world.

How they behave
You have to back up
your 'summing–up'
words' with examples
that explain what
you mean.

Exercise B

1 Go back to the first person you described in Exercise A. Think about
what their character might be like. Make a list of words to describe
what they are like as people.

2 Now do the same thing for the second person you chose in Exercise A.

LISA investigates adjectives

LISA's job today is to find out about adjectives. She has fed in to her computer a short extract from a story. All the adjectives are printed in orange, like this. All the nouns are printed in blue, like this.

> My friends. I thought about them. Hazel Brent is my best friend. She has black, curly hair, bright, black eyes, and very white teeth in a nut-brown face. She is always laughing.

Exercise A

LISA wants you to explain to her:

1. Exactly what are adjectives?

2. What other type of word are they used with in these examples?

3. Which comes first?

4. What kind of information do adjectives give us?

Write down your answers to these questions.

Exercise B

This description comes from another story. It has been split into separate sentences. After each sentence you are told how many adjectives it contains. Write them down.

1. Spit Nolan was a pal of mine. (0)

2. He was a thin lad with a bony face that was always pale, except for two rosy spots on his cheekbones. (4)

3. He had quick brown eyes, short, wiry hair, rather stooped shoulders, and we all knew that he had only one lung. (5)

Exercise C

Make a list with three columns headed 'Subjects', 'Nouns' and 'Adjectives'. Write the numbers 1–10 on the left. For each of the following sentences:

- write down the subject
- write down any nouns in it
- write down any adjectives in it.

1. We arrived at the station in plenty of time.

2. The train had not yet arrived.

3. We walked along the platform.

4. My young sister Donna was with us.

5. Donna is five.

6. An impatient traveller pushed past us.

7. My sister was knocked over.

8. Her new coat was completely spoiled.

9. The stupid, rude man didn't even say 'Sorry'.

10. At last the train arrived.

More about adjectives

Exercise A

LISA thought she had adjectives completely worked out. Now her computer has worked out that *they can be used in two different ways!* It has collected some sentences that show this. Can you help **LISA** work it out? To help you **the adjectives are in orange** and **the nouns are in blue**.

Sentences

1 I have a young brother.
2 Sometimes he is naughty.
3 He throws his food on the clean floor.
4 He seems happy when he does this.
5 Mum looks angry.

What to do

1 Sort the sentences into two groups:
   A: ones where the adjective is used with a noun
   B: ones where it is used in some other way.

2 Write an explanation of how the adjectives in Group B are used.

Turning nouns into adjectives

We can turn some nouns into adjectives by adding to the ends of them:

+ish	+less	+ful
child ➡ childish	hope ➡ hopeless	hope ➡ hopeful

Turning adjectives into nouns

We can turn some adjectives into nouns by adding to the ends of them:

+ness	+ity
happy ➡ happiness	sane ➡ sanity

Exercise B

Turn each of the following nouns into an adjective by adding to the end of it. Some of the nouns can be made into more than one adjective.

1 help   6 faith
2 fool   7 cheer
3 fright   8 sheep
4 wish   9 success
5 kitten   10 peace

Exercise C

Some of the following adjectives can be turned into nouns by adding *-ness*. Which ones?

1 deaf   6 careful
2 bold   7 weary
3 elastic   8 bent
4 cheap   9 brave
5 clever   10 wicked

Using adjectives to describe people

On this page you will see how fiction writers use adjectives to describe their characters. Both the extracts come from full-length stories.

Exercise A

In this description some of the adjectives have been removed. They are listed at the end of it. Write down the number of each blank and the adjective that should go in it:

I turned around and looked at him. He had on bright __1__ pants, a red-green-and-white plaid jacket, and a __2__ green shirt. I'm six foot one and he came up to my shoulder. He was __3__ , and he wore these __4__ glasses with a hearing aid attached. He was puffing on a __5__ cigarette, the kind smokers use when they first give up the habit. The cigarette glowed red when he breathed in on it. I figured he was about fifty, and I could smell a __6__ __7__ cologne or after-shave he had on.

Adjectives

sweet	bald	sickly
fake	red	yellow-tinted
bright		

Exercise B

This short description comes from the story 'The Monster Garden' by Vivien Alcock. This time it isn't a person she's describing! Read it through and write down a word to fit each of the spaces:

The monster sat on the pillow and stared at me with its __1__ eyes. It had changed again. It was now – most horribly, grotesquely – half human in shape. It had a __2__ head, but no hair, no nose, no ears. It had two eyes and a __3__ slit of a mouth, as if someone had drawn a line in __4__ clay with a knife; a __5__ body, __6__ __7__ arms and legs. But no hands or feet. Its __8__ flesh had a __9__ tinge. It looked absurdly like a very __10__ jelly-baby.

All the words you have written down should be adjectives.

Writer's notebooks

When writers begin to think about the stories they are going to write they often keep a notebook in which they jot down the ideas they have. On this page we have made up three pages from writers' notebooks. What you have to do is to turn these sets of notes into complete descriptions. Each set of notes should build up into a set of complete sentences.

What to do

1   Look at the first group of words in Extract A. Make up one or two sentences that use all the words in the notes, like this:

small – face like a rat – teeth grey

He was a small ratty-faced man with grey teeth.

2   Now do the same for each group of words in the extract.
3   When you have finished Extract A, go on to Extract B and then Extract C.

Extract A

small – face like a rat – teeth grey
eyes: dark – quick – clever – like a rat's
ears: slightly pointed at top
cloth cap – greyish jacket –
enormous pockets
grey jacket + quick eyes + pointed ears –
looked like huge human rat

Extract B

dirty white shorts – not wearing anything else
body burnt dark (sun)
hair tousled – feet dusty (like chalk)
arm stretched out – flute in open hand
thin – bony legs – strong (body wiry + hard)

Extract C

<u>Dr Spencer</u>
hands, feet + round face – all tiny
brown – wrinkled – like shrivelled apple
like old elf – hair white, wispy – steel-rimmed glasses
quick eye – flashing smile – talked fast

Writing a description of somebody

Now it's time to put what you have been learning into practice. You are going to write a short description of somebody. Follow the instructions below.

1 Choosing a subject
Decide who you are going to describe. It can be a real person, someone you have made up, or a person based on one of the pictures on page 29. Think carefully and get a clear picture of the person in your mind's eye.

2 Collecting words
Look at the headings and lists of words on this page. Collect words for each of the headings (Face, Hair, etc.):
- Take words you like from the lists.
- Add words of your own.

Resources: words

Face

fat	heavy	narrow	oval	round	square	thin

Hair

auburn	balding	black	blonde	braided	brown	crew-cut	cropped
curly	dyed	long	short	straight	thick	thin	wavy

Eyes

beady	blue	blue-grey	dim	green	grey	grey-green
hazel	milky	piercing				

Nose

large	long	pointed	flat	prominent	short	small	snub

Mouth and lips

down-turned	fleshy	full	mean	pouting	smiling	thin

Jaw

fleshy	jutting	receding	square	strong	weak

Hands and fingers

thin	wrinkled	fine	fat	heavy	muscular	elegant	ugly
tapering	stumpy	square	pointed				

Body

chunky	fat	lanky	podgy	scrawny	short	skinny	slender
slim	squat	stocky	stout	tall	thickset	thin	willowy

Personality

awkward	bad-tempered	boisterous	bold	brave	careful	cheerful	crabby
easy-going	excitable	friendly	funny	generous	happy	kind	mean
miserable	nervous	nervy	rash	rude	sad	sensitive	serious
shy	solemn	starry-eyed	sunny	thoughtful	timid	tough	uncaring

3 Writing sentences

Now write at least two sentences about *each* of these:

- head/face
- hair
- hands and fingers
- body
- personality.

Use some of the sentences below and make up some of your own.

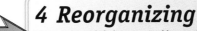

4 Reorganizing

You should have a list of at least ten sentences. They probably aren't in the best order. Decide:

- what order they should be in
- if you need to add any more sentences to complete the description.

5 Rewriting and checking

Now write out your final version, making sure that it is neat and clear.
When you have finished, check it carefully for mistakes in:

- grammar
- punctuation
- spelling.

Resources: sentences

Head, face, hair

His/her head was ——————————————— .
S/he had ——————— eyes that ——————— .
When you looked at his/her face, ——————— .

Hands and fingers

His/her hands looked ——————————————— .
S/he moved his/her hands in a ——————— way.
As s/he spoke, s/he ——————— his/her hands/fingers.

Body

S/he was rather ——————— and ——————— .
When s/he moved, his/her body was ——————— .

Personality

To me s/he was a ——————— person.
Most of the time s/he was ——————— , but
sometimes s/he could be ——————— .

Summing up

S/he was just like a ——————— .
If s/he'd been a car, she would have been a ——————— ,
because s/he ——————— .

How?
Different ways of writing

There are four main kinds of writing we can do:

- we can **describe** what someone or something is like
- we can **tell a story**
- we can **explain** things
- we can **argue**.

In this unit we have been studying **how to write a description**. We shall look at the other three kinds of writing in the next unit.

Nouns and adjectives

Some nouns can be turned into adjectives and some adjectives can be turned into nouns:

Turning nouns into adjectives
We can turn some nouns into adjectives by adding to the ends of them.

+ish
child ➡ *childish*

+less
hope ➡ *hopeless*

+ful
hope ➡ *hopeful*

Turning adjectives into nouns
We can turn some adjectives into nouns by adding to the ends of them.

+ness   +ity
kind ➡ *kindness*   *sane* ➡ *sanity*

Adjectives

Adjectives are sometimes called 'describing words'. We can use them in two ways:

Adjectives with nouns
We use adjectives before nouns. They give more information about the noun:

- a car
- a new car
- a new red car
- a new shiny red car.

All the words in orange are adjectives.

Adjectives to tell us more about subjects
We also use adjectives in sentences after verbs like 'be'. They come after the verb and tell us more about the subject of the sentence:

My car   *is*   *red*.
Subject   **Verb** **Adjective**

Describing people

A description of a person can include information about:

- face
- hair
- eyes
- nose
- mouth and lips
- jaw
- hands and fingers
- body
- personality.

Pages 34 and 35 have useful word lists and sentence frameworks to use when writing a description of a person.

LISA reads the papers

In the last unit **LISA** was interviewed by the press. She wants to find out what newspapers are like and what they are for. Then she will be able to report back to Planet K48Z46 what she has found out.

Discussion points
- Do you regularly have a newspaper at home?
- If so, which one(s)?
- Why do people read papers?

In this unit you will learn about:

Language awareness
The language of newspapers:
- stories
- explanations
- opinions and arguments.

Sentence grammar
Verbs in the sentence: where they come and what they do.

Grammar and sentences
How we use verbs in sentences.

Drafting and writing:
- building up a story by answering questions
- using different verbs to describe action
- rewriting sentences to make a better story.

Stories and explanations

LISA has discovered that newspapers tell us about all kinds of things. But they only contain a small number of different kinds of writing. The commonest of these is **stories**:

> Mum Ranjan Parmar lowered her children to safety from their blazing house yesterday with a makeshift rope of saris.
> The 34-year-old tied the five Indian outfits together. She anchored them to a bed.
> Then she eased the kids, Ajay, seven, and Hitarth, three, to the ground.

Newspapers also have to explain things to their readers, so they contain a lot of **explanations**:

> Only 16 per cent of women are naturally fair haired – with most blondes getting their hair colour out of a bottle. They spend £125 million a year on dyes. Before they resort to the bottle exactly half Britain's women are brunettes and nearly a fifth are going grey.

Exercise A

Write down whether each of these extracts is a story or an explanation.

1 Five stray peacocks who brought mayhem to a Cotswold village have finally been rounded up. Villager Sue Chick managed to trap the noisy birds ...

2 Allergy to peanuts has doubled in 10 years. Today, one person in 100 will suffer and, of all allergies, it is the one most likely to be fatal.

3 Your hair *can* be your crowning glory – but only if you know how to manage it. The key to finding the right hairstyle is not to repeat the shape of your face.

Exercise B

This time, work out *just from these headlines* whether the article that followed was a story or an explanation:

1 Death row pet wins his appeal

2 How a cricket ball moves off the seam

3 Express trains miss crashing by seconds

Opinions and arguments

Newspapers contain a third kind of writing. For example, one newspaper reported that the original teddy bear on which the Winnie the Pooh stories were based is kept in a New York library. Then the reporter wrote the extract on the right:

This isn't a story, and it isn't an explanation. It is an opinion. You find **opinions** – and **arguments**:

- in the opinion columns
- on the letters page
- and in other places in the newspaper.

Bear necessity

There is no doubt about it. Winnie the Pooh must be brought back to Britain from New York. The Americans will surely allow that if we pay the right price. How about offering them a jar of honey?

Exercise A

Write down whether each of these extracts is a story or an explanation or an opinion:

 'Don't mark homework – it upsets dunces,' says top education expert.

 Goldfish were domesticated by the Chinese 1,000 years ago and introduced to Britain in the early 18th century. There are more than 125 recognized breeds and they are the most popular children's pet, with 14 per cent of households having them.

 Film producers were accused yesterday of bad taste for using lookalikes to portray Princes William and Harry. As shooting began on a TV film about their mother's life, Prince Charles was said to be 'uneasy' about the way it focuses on his sons.

 It is bad enough that anyone should want to cash in on Princess Diana's death by rushing out a low-budget television film about her life but the intention to involve her sons – using lookalikes to play them – shows even greater lack of taste.

Exercise B

LISA is finding newspapers quite difficult to understand. One of the reasons is that they use a number of words she has not met before. Help her out by writing an explanation of what each of these words means:

- **mayhem** (page 38 Exercise A number 1)
- **allergies** (page 38 Exercise A number 2)
- **Death row** (page 38 Exercise B number 1)
- **lookalikes** (page 39 Exercise A number 4)

Teaching LISA about verbs

Now it's time for **LISA's** computer to learn about verbs. She has fed in a newspaper story with the **verbs** marked in **red** and the <u>subjects</u> underlined in <u>green</u>:

Mum <u>Ranjan Parmar</u> lowered her children to safety from their blazing house yesterday with a makeshift rope of saris. <u>The 34-year-old</u> tied the five Indian outfits together. <u>She</u> anchored them to a bed. Then <u>she</u> eased the kids, Ajay, seven, and Hitarth, three, to the ground.

Exercise A

Look at the sentences in the story above. How would you explain to **LISA** what a verb is? Write two sentences:

1 telling her what kind of thing verbs tell us

2 telling us where the verbs come in these sentences.

When you have finished (*and not before!*), look at **What is a verb?** on page 46. Compare your answer with what it says there.

Exercise B

Write down the verb in each of the following sentences:

1 Two trains nearly crashed yesterday.

2 It happened near Southall.

3 One of the trains went through a red light.

4 Both trains used their emergency braking systems.

5 They halted about a hundred yards apart.

Exercise C

Write down the subject and the verb in each of the following sentences:

1 Every year our family spends Christmas in Manchester.

2 We stay with my grandad.

3 He lives in a large house on the outskirts of the city.

4 The house has lots of rooms and a large garden.

5 It has six bedrooms.

6 So all the children have their own bedroom.

7 Sometimes we stay with grandad in the summer, too.

8 In summer we play football and cricket in the garden.

9 I really enjoy my visits to grandad's.

10 Grandad enjoys our visits, too.

More about verbs

Exercise A

On the right is a page of notes one of **LISA's** friends made in her diary during a summer holiday. Write one sentence describing what she did each day (five sentences altogether). Underline the verb in each one.

☐	<u>Monday</u>	to beach
☐	<u>Tuesday</u>	visit to Ramsay Island
☐	<u>Wednesday</u>	car to Hallam Castle
☐	<u>Thursday</u>	shops in Atherton
☐	<u>Friday</u>	home
☐		

Exercise B

Professor Idiottprooff is an inventor. He lives a very strange life.
The set of pictures below shows you what he does on weekdays. Look at the pictures and then follow the instructions at the bottom of the page.

Monday
Wednesday
Tuesday
Thursday
Friday

What to do

1 Write one sentence for each day of the week, describing what the professor does that day. Start with these words:
On ___ days the professor ...

2 When you have finished, go through your sentences and:
  ○ underline the verb
  ◉ put a ring round the subject.

Using verbs

Each of the sentences you were looking at on the last two pages had one verb – *and it was only one word*. The verb in a sentence may be made up of more than one word. In the sentences on the right the verbs are underlined in red:

Later on we shall look at how these verbs work. For now you just need to be able to spot them.

> Five stray peacocks brought mayhem to a Cotswold village. Now they have been rounded up. Villager Sue Chick managed to trap the noisy birds.

Exercise A

The texts on this page are taken from a true newspaper story. In the first section below some of the verbs have been cut out. They are listed underneath the extract – with a lot of other verbs that don't belong in the story. Write down the number of each space and the verb that should go in it.

Tapes __1__ yesterday of the tense last minutes of the 22-minute ordeal of the man with no flying experience who __2__ a light aircraft when the pilot, his future father-in-law, __3__ of a heart attack.

Alan Anderson, 24, of Llantwit Major, South Glamorgan, __4__ to a near-perfect landing at Cardiff airport by a pilot instructor flying alongside. Mr Anderson was last night recovering from deep shock. His mother, Carol Anderson, said he __5__ never to fly again.

Verbs

had vowed	disappeared
said	was guided
died	would be assisted
escaped	was forced to land
were released	wanted

Exercise B

This time there is no help. Work out a suitable verb to go in each space and write them down.

Clue: they are all one-word verbs.

The instructor, Robert Legg, 26, __6__ to Mr Anderson's mayday call, __7__ and caught up with Mr Anderson's aircraft at 2,000 ft above Penarth, near Cardiff.

An amateur radio enthusiast, Howard Done, __8__ the pair speaking in the tense moments immediately before landing:

ANDERSON: I can see you.
LEGG: OK ... Just __9__ to my instructions ... take the throttle and pull it slightly out until the RPM __10__ down to about 2,300.
ANDERSON: Well, which __11__ the throttle?
LEGG: There should be a black lever in the centre of the panel ... That's fine. Let the aeroplane fly itself.
ANDERSON: I __12__ it would.

Twenty killed as jet slices cable car wires

Exercise A

In the first part of the newspaper story below, a number of verbs have been cut out. The missing verbs are listed on the left with others which do not belong in the text. Write down the number of each blank and the verb you think should fill it.

Verbs
said
injured
had tried to fly
were said to be
complained
was hurt
flew
had worked
slashed
believed
were working
offered
could give

A LOW-FLYING JET yesterday ___1___ through the wires supporting an alpine cable car lift, sending at least twenty people plunging to their deaths in the valley below.

Rescue teams ___2___ last night under arc lights to remove the bodies from the mangled yellow car near the ski resort of Cavalese. All but one of the victims ___3___ foreign tourists. None of the crew of the United States military aircraft ___4___.

Policeman Robert Cavada in Cavalese ___5___ at least six of the victims were Germans. RAI state television said two were Hungarian, and two Polish. Officials said a child was among the dead but ___6___ no more details.

Exercise B

In this part of the story, the verb is given but it is not in the correct form. Write down the number of the blank and the correct form of the verb.

THE ACCIDENT ___7___ (take) place on the first leg of the cable lift which ___8___ (rise) three miles to the peak of Monte Cermis in the Dolomites. This ___9___ (be) also the scene of Italy's worst cable car accident in 1976 in which more than 40 people died.

The aircraft, a Grumman Prowler packed with electronic warfare equipment, ___10___ (rip) through the cables of the lift in mid-afternoon. The car on which the victims ___11___ (travel) fell more than 300 feet.

According to one report the plane actually ___12___ (brush) the car. But a local hotelier told the news agency Ansa last night that the plane ___13___ (hit) the cables with its tail fin as it flew under them. US sources confirmed the aircraft suffered minor tail damage.

'The pilot was apparently unaware that he ___14___ (strike) a cable or injured anyone,' the US defence secretary, William Cohen, told the Senate armed services committee in Washington. A Cavalese fireman said, 'I ___15___ (see) the aircraft go to and fro at a very low level. They do it every day and we ___16___ (protest) on numerous occasions, but with no result.'

How did it happen?

On this page and the next we are going to build up a story. We shall focus on how to use verbs when telling a story.

The picture on the right shows you how the story ended. We are going to imagine that this story actually happened to you – so you will tell it as 'I'.

There are three columns below. On the left there are pictures showing what happened. In the middle there are questions. **Answer each question using at least one complete sentence.** On the right there are lists of verbs. **Use at least one of these verbs in each sentence.**

1 How did the story start: what were you doing?	1 stride jog roam	stride saunter wander	amble potter
2 What was your dog doing?	2 tug jerk	strain haul	drag heave

3 What happened to the lead?	3 snap break come apart	part split	sever
4 What happened to the dog?	4 tumble crash plummet	descend plunge	dive topple
5 What happened to you?	5 trip tumble fall headlong	stumble overbalance	sprawl

6 What did you do?	6 peer hunt	observe look for	seek
7 What happened to the edge of the cliff?	7 shatter break off	crumble come away	splinter disintegrate

	8 What happened to you?	8	plunge	topple	crash
			career	plummet	
			roll	slither	

	9 What stopped your fall?	9	stop	break	check
			catch	block	
	10 What did you see when you looked up?	10	see	notice	spot
			observe	gaze	recognize
	11 How were you saved?	11	rescue	assist	
			help	save	

Redrafting

You should now have at least eleven sentences. At the moment they are just answers to questions. If you take the questions away the answers may not make much sense on their own. In addition, you may need to add more details to make the story better.

1 Look at each sentence carefully. Does it make sense on its own? If not, rewrite it so that it does.

2 Now look again. Are there any details you could add to each sentence to make it more informative and interesting? Add them now.

3 Now look at the sentences as a whole. Do they add up to a story? Do you need to write more sentences to make your story clearer and more exciting? Write them now.

> 1   It snapped
>   ↓
>   The lead snapped
>
> 2   ↓
>   Suddenly, without any warning, the lead snapped.
>
> 3   Suddenly, without any warning, the lead snapped.
>
>   He plunged over the edge of the cliff.
>
>   Now there was nothing holding Scotty back.

Writing a final version

By now your work probably looks a mess. You need to write a fresh copy with all the alterations included. As you write, make sure that you correct mistakes in:

● grammar   ● punctuation   ● spelling.

Summing up what you've learned

Different kinds of writing

There are four basic kinds of writing:

- **Story**
  A story tells what happened over a period of time: 'First this happened and then that happened.'
- **Explanation**
  An explanation explains what things are like, or how they work.
- **Opinion and argument**
  An opinion expresses what a person thinks or believes. An argument usually gives an opinion plus the reasons for it.

In this unit you have looked at these three kinds of writing. In the previous unit you looked at the fourth kind of writing:

- **Description**
  A description tells us about the appearance of something – what it looks like and what it *is* like.

Drafting a story

1. One way of building up a story is to ask yourself a set of **questions** about it:
   - What happened first?
   - Why did it happen?
   - What did it feel like?
   - What happened next?
   and so on.

2. In any story verbs are very important – especially **verbs that describe action**. So you should take trouble to choose the best verb for each action. *Don't be satisfied with the first verb you think of.*

3. Always take time to **rewrite your sentences**. Make sure that they:
   - make sense on their own
   - fit in well with the sentences that come before and after
   - don't miss out important information.

What is a verb?

- A verb is a part of a sentence.
- In a statement sentence it normally comes after the subject.

We use verbs:

- to describe **actions**
  He *tumbled* over the edge.
- to describe **feelings and states of mind**
  I *love* sausage and chips for breakfast.

The verb in a sentence can be:

- **one word**
  He *tumbled* over the edge.
- **a group of words**
  I *have been thinking* about that.

Guidebook for visitors

LISA has been given the job of preparing a guidebook to this new planet she is exploring. It will include an introduction to the English language. You have been asked to help her make a list of the words and sentences that foreign visitors will find most useful.

She also has to explain some of the grammar she has been learning. You are going to help her with that, too.

In this unit you will revise:

Words and phrases:
- ⦿ about school
- ⦿ about people
- ⦿ for stories and actions.

Different kinds of sentence

Subjects, nouns and pronouns

Nouns and adjectives

Verbs

Language and life

LISA's dictionary and phrase book

School

In **Unit Two** we saw **LISA** at school. She learned a lot of words and sentences to help her find her way around the school.

People

In **Unit Three** we looked at ways of describing what people look like, how they behave and what their personalities are like.

Stories and activities

In **Unit Four** the focus was on telling stories and describing actions.

Exercise A

1 Make a list of the twenty words you think would be most useful to a foreign visitor to your school.

2 Choose the five most useful of these. Write a clear explanation of what each one means. (Remember that you can't take it for granted that the visitor knows anything at all about schools.)

Exercise B

3 Think of three questions it would be really useful for your visitor to be able to ask. Write them down.

4 Think of three directives (instructions, orders) they should understand. Write them down.

Exercise C

5 Make a list of five adjectives that are useful when describing a person's face.

6 Now do the same for each of the following:
- eyes
- hands and fingers
- body
- personality.

Exercise D

7 Your visitor wants to be able to find out what a particular person looks like (their appearance). Write three questions they could ask to get this information: a yes/no question, an either/or question, and a question-word question.

8 Now do the same for questions about someone's personality: make up three questions, one of each kind.

Exercise E

9 Some visitors have difficulty finding suitable verbs to describe movement. Help them by making lists of verbs for each of the following:
- walking
- pulling
- breaking
- falling.

10 Many public notices use action verbs. They often contain directive sentences (orders, or commands) – for example: 'Keep off the grass.' Write three directive sentences that visitors need to understand as they visit public places.

Different kinds of sentence

Exercise A

LISA knows that there are three different kinds of sentence. She has examples of all three in this short conversation:

A: *Don't go into the classroom.*

B: *Why can't I go in there?*

A: *Mrs Green is in there.*

1 What are the three types of sentence called?

2 For each type of sentence:
  a explain when we use it
  b give an example from the conversation
  c give an example of your own.

Exercise B

LISA knows there are three different kinds of question. She has collected these examples of them:

A: *Do you like English lessons?*

B: *Do you prefer English lessons or maths lessons?*

C: *Which lessons do you like best?*

1 **a** What do we call questions like **A**?
  b Give another example of this type of question.

2 **a** What do we call questions like **B**?
  b Give another example of this type of question.

3 **a** What do we call questions like **C**?
  b Give another example of this type of question.
  c This type of question can begin with a number of words. **Which** is one of them. Write down two more.

Exercise C

LISA has remembered that we can use directives for many different purposes. She has listed these purposes for using directives:

- to invite
- to order or command
- to beg or plead
- to wish someone well
- to advise
- to warn
- to ask or request.

She needs help with examples. Write an example of each of these directives.

Subjects, nouns and pronouns

Exercise A

Help **LISA** by writing down the subjects of these sentences:

1. It was raining cats and dogs last night.
2. Peter and Mary decided to go to see their friends Jan and Dave.
3. Unfortunately their friends were out.
4. They were not pleased.

But what is a subject?

LISA needs to write a short explanation of what a subject is. What should she write? Include information about these points:

- where the subject comes in a statement sentence
- what it tells us
- what form it can take (one word? many words? what kind of word?).

Exercise B

Now **LISA** has to find examples of nouns and explain what they are. These are the sentences she has chosen:

A: *I have visited many foreign countries, but I have never been to Australia.*

B: *I should love to visit Queensland and its famous Barrier Reef.*

C: *Of course Australia is famous for its coast-line and beaches.*

1. Write down all the nouns in the three sentences.
2. Give two examples each (so four altogether) of:
   - a common noun
   - a proper noun.
3. Explain:
   - what a common noun is
   - what a proper noun is.

Exercise C

LISA knows that pronouns refer back to something we've already mentioned. Can you help her by answering these questions:

1. Why do we use them?
2. What kind of thing do they refer back to?

LISA has started making a list of the personal pronouns. Can you help her out by writing down the missing pronouns?

I/me
__1__ / __2__
you
she/her
__3__ / __4__
__5__
they/them

Nouns and adjectives

Exercise A

Now **LISA** has to find examples of adjectives and explain what they are. These are the sentences she has chosen:

A: *Your new pen is fantastic!*

B: *My aunt Edie bought it for me in that big shop at the far end of the High Street.*

C: *They've got different kinds of pens.*

D: *I like this one because I do italic writing.*

1 Write down all the adjectives in the four sentences.

2 Help **LISA** by writing an explanation of adjectives:
- where we use them in a sentence

   Note: adjectives can be used in two different ways. Make sure that you explain this properly.
- what they are for.

Exercise B

LISA wants to explain how to turn:
- nouns into adjectives and
- adjectives into nouns.

1 Write an explanation of how we do each of these things.

2 For each explanation give two examples. There are lists of suitable nouns and adjectives below to help you.

Nouns to turn into adjectives

brute	colour	grace
lad	self	faith

Adjectives to turn into nouns

artful	stupid	weary
dark	elastic	sane

Verbs

Exercise A

LISA has collected these sample sentences. The verb in each one is only one word. Help her by writing down the verb in each sentence.

1. Today Julia celebrated her twelfth birthday.
2. Her parents gave her a new bike.
3. Her brother had no spare money.
4. He just sent her a card.
5. Julia understands.
6. Sometimes she has no money either.
7. In the evening the whole family went to the cinema.
8. Julia went to bed tired but happy.

Exercise B

In the following newspaper report some of the verbs have been missed out. The missing verbs are listed at the bottom in the wrong order. Write down the number of each blank and the verb that should go in it.

Mankind __1__ another giant leap in exploring space yesterday. Scientists __2__ the discovery of millions of tons of life-giving water hidden as ice beneath the surface of the Moon. The find __3__ that a permanent manned lunar base could be operating within thirty years. The Moon __4__ a vast launching pad for missions to Mars and the rest of the solar system. The dramatic news __5__ back to Earth by NASA's unmanned Lunar Prospector probe. It __6__ the ice in vast, dark craters at the Moon's north and south poles, far from the reach of the sun.

Verbs

revealed   detected
took   was beamed
means   could become

Exercise C

In each of the following sentences the verb is given but not in the correct form. Write down the number of the sentence and the correct form of the verb.

1. Today we _____ (start) our half-term holiday.
2. Some of the class _____ (go) away for a holiday.
3. My brother and I _____ (plan) to stay at home.
4. We _____ (want) to make a new kite.
5. We _____ (construct) it of aluminium and nylon.
6. The weather forecast _____ (promise) high winds all week.
7. The kite _____ (need) to be very strong.
8. We _____ (hope) to fly it on Thursday.

LISA has collected a number of cuttings. They are printed on this page and the next. She is using these extracts to explain how English speakers behave and how they use language. Unfortunately she has made a number of mistakes. Look at each extract carefully and then answer the questions that go with it.

Extract A

LISA says:

'This is part of a family Christmas card. These are cards earth people send each other on special occasions to ask for presents.'

Questions

1 Who is the card written by and who is it for?

2 How do you know?

3 Where does it come from?

4 How do you know?

5 What do you think of **LISA's** definition of a Christmas card and why?

Saturday

Arrived on Tuesday. Fantastic hotel right by the beach.

Great weather – sunny all day and very hot! Mum sends her love. We're both sitting by the pool soaking up the sun.

Lots of love,

Dad

Extract B

LISA says:

'This is a description of a new form of robot transportation being tried out on earth.'

Questions

1 Where does the extract come from?

2 What is wrong with **LISA's** description of it?

3 What kind of writing is this:
- story
- description
- explanation
- opinion/argument
- a mixture?

The plane that flew solo

CAROL HALL looked out of her office window in the little airport near Urbana, Ohio, and wondered what was going on. A yellow, single-engine plane was taxiing along the runway, apparently ready for take off, except that it narrowly missed another aircraft that was coming in to land.

'We couldn't figure out what the pilot was trying to do,' said Ms Hall.

A moment later, she found the answer, as the distraught pilot burst into her office, grabbed the telephone and called the emergency services. His plane had taken off without him.

Extract C

LISA says:

'This is from a newspaper. It is a news report giving information about a new form of transport. It is very cheap – it only costs ten pounds. That is why there are so many cars on the roads.'

Questions

1. Does it come from a newspaper?

2. What are the reasons for your answer?

3. Is it a news report or something else?

4. How do you know?

5. What is the audience for this extract?

6. What do you think of the last two sentences **LISA** says about it?

Test drive a Proton. £10 says you'll love it.

Extract D

LISA says:

'This is from an encyclopaedia (a big information book) for experts on history. As you can see, these experts only know a small number of words and have only a small knowledge of history.'

Questions

1. Is she right?

2. If not, who is this written for?

3. Why do you think so?

4. What is the **purpose** of this text?

5. What kind of writing is it:
   - story
   - description
   - explanation
   - opinion/argument
   - a mixture?

The most famous tombs were pyramids, built for the Pharaohs and their families. They were buried with masses of gold, jewels, furniture, statues, even models of servants – everything they needed in the next world. These were rich pickings for tomb robbers. So later tombs were cut deep into the cliffs for safety. It didn't work! These were robbed, too.

Time to celebrate

LISA wants to experience every aspect of life on earth. So she is investigating what we do at Christmas time.

LISA's version

Imagine that you are **LISA**. Write five or six sentences explaining to the creatures of her planet what the Christmas holiday is and how humans celebrate it. Remember that **LISA** has not been told anything about Christmas, so it all seems very strange to her, and she may not get it right!

Your explanation

Think about how you would explain the Christmas holiday to **LISA**. You could include these points in your explanation:

- why people started celebrating Christmas
- why they celebrate it now
- what they do.

Write about ten sentences.

LISA learns to cook ... and other things

Of course androids don't need to eat or drink. **LISA** finds it difficult to understand why human beings spend so much time poking food into their mouths. Why can't they just swallow a few pills?

- Do you enjoy eating?
- What are your favourite foods?
- What would we miss out on if we only needed to take pills to live?
- What would the advantages be?
- If you could live by just taking 'food pills', would you like to?

In this unit you will learn about:

The language of food:

- special words
- how we write about the same thing for different people and different purposes
- using directive sentences.

Pronouns

Sentence objects:

- what they are
- how we use them.

How to write instructions

Talking about food

Exercise A

LISA finds it difficult to understand the different ways in which people talk about food. She has collected some examples and would like your help in answering these questions about each one. Write down your answers.

1 Who is the extract written for? How do you know?

2 What is the purpose of the writing:
- to give information
- to persuade you to do something – or to change the way you think
- to provide entertainment
- some other purpose – if so, what?

Extract A

Bombay Potatoes

Potatoes
1-2 tablespoons of Curry Paste for each pound of potatoes
Mix curry paste with a little oil and then add to potatoes.
(sprinkle a little salt if desired.)
Bake in oven as for roast potatoes 1½ (approx.) hours.
NB Boil potatoes for a shorter cooking time.

Extract B

My grandparents were poor, really poor.

When you are poor, you become ingenious. You get a nose for a bargain, and you experiment. You become original, and some of the best dishes in the world are the fruit of poverty. You search through cookery books trying to find out how to make scraps delectable, and how far you can stretch a slice of beef before it becomes transparent.

The food of poverty in Eastern Europe where my grandparents came from was potatoes, as in Ireland. Potato pancakes were eaten with pickled cucumber, with apple sauce, and even with mashed potato. After that you could eat them with sugar or apricot jam as a sweet. In German they were called Kartoffeln Pfuffer. In Yiddish they had the less unwieldy name of latkes. The ingredients are cheap; they are easy to make and yet a delicacy.

Glossary
ingenious – inventive
delectable – delicious
before it becomes transparent – before you can see through it

Extract C

Cod, chips, peas £3.95
Gammon steak, pineapple, chips £4.25
Egg, sausage, chips £3.25
Portion of chips 75 p

Extract D

Fisherman's Supper

Succulent nuggets of cod lightly fried in the Chef's special beer batter, accompanied by French fries and garden fresh petits pois.

£7.50

Recipes

Exercise A

This recipe was written for adults. You want to find out if it is suitable for 8-year-olds. Look at it carefully and write down the answers to these questions:

1 Look at the words the writer uses. Are there any words there that 8-year-old children might find difficult? If so, write them down and write an explanation of them, or find an easier word.

2 Are there any sentences that these readers might find difficult? If so, write them down and explain why they are difficult.

Angel cake

2 oz plain flour	6½ oz caster sugar
6 egg whites	pinch of salt
¾ teaspoon cream of tartar	3 drops of vanilla essence
2 drops of almond essence	

8–9-inch diameter angel cake tin (with funnelled base)

Method

Set oven at 375°F or Mark 5. Sift the flour and 3½oz caster sugar three times and set on one side. Place the egg whites, salt and cream of tartar in a large, dry basin and whisk with a rotary beater until foamy.

Add the remaining sugar, 2 tablespoons at a time, and the essences and continue beating until the mixture will stand in peaks. Carefully fold in the sifted flour and sugar. Turn the mixture into the clean, dry tin, level the surface and draw a knife through to break any air bubbles. Bake the cake in the pre-set oven for 30–35 minutes or until no imprint remains when your finger lightly touches the top.

When cake is ready, turn it upside down on a wire rack and leave until quite cold, when the cake will fall easily from the tin.

Serve plain for tea or with fruit for a lunch party. Pull into pieces with two forks rather than cut with a knife as the texture is very delicate.

Exercise B

Now look at the recipe on the right.

1 Where do you think it comes from?

2 Who do you think it was written for?

3 Can you read and understand it?

4 What makes it more difficult to understand than the other recipe? (Careful: there's more than one answer to this question!)

5 If you wanted to write this recipe so that primary school children could understand it, what would you have to do?

RICH ORANGE GINGERBREAD

4oz soft brown sugar	10oz golden syrup
4oz marg.	2oz mixed peel
grated rind 1 orange	½tsp bicarb of soda
8oz sifted plain flour	4 tablesp. milk
2 eggs	3tsp. gr. ginger

1. Cream marg & sugar with orange rind till light and fluffy.
2. Beat in one egg w. one tbsp. flour - repeat with 2nd egg.
3. Sift remaining flour with ginger & stir into creamed mixture w. golden syrup (warmed if nec.) & mixed peel.
4. Dissolve bicarb in milk & stir in.
5. Mix well & bake in well-greased 8" square cake tin (Gas 8 or 325F.) for about 1½ hours Keep for few days before cutting

The language of recipes

You have probably noticed that recipes contain a lot of **directive sentences**. These are sentences that give instructions or orders. Usually they start with the **verb** and don't have a subject. The verbs are in **red**.

- **Sift** the flour.
- **Add** the egg.
- **Mix** them together.

Exercise A
Look back at the recipes on page 59. Find and write down five directive sentences.

Objects

Exercise B
LISA has discovered that a lot of English sentences contain something called an **object**. In this recipe she has underlined some of the objects in purple. The verbs are printed in **red**.

> **Sprinkle** flour on the worktop. **Roll** out the dough. **Cut** it into shapes. **Put** them in the oven.

Now LISA needs help in answering these questions:

1. Where does the object come in the sentence?

2. Is it one word, more than one word, or either?

3. If it is one word, what kinds of word can be the object of the sentence?

Exercise C
Write down the objects in each of these sentences:

1. Get some butter and sugar.
2. Beat them together.
3. Sift the flour.
4. Add the egg and the vanilla.
5. Add a pinch of salt.
6. Mix them.
7. Roll the dough in your hands.
8. Make a big ball.
9. Cover it with clingfilm.

Exercise D
All the sentences you have been looking at so far are directives. But you can find objects in statement sentences, too. What is the object in each of these sentences?

1. My friend loves biscuits.
2. She often eats them.
3. I like cakes and biscuits.
4. Most of all I like vanilla ice cream.
5. But I can't stand marzipan.

More about pronouns

Exercise A

Let's see how much you can remember about personal pronouns. In this extract there are *eight* personal pronouns. Read the extract and then answer the questions that follow.

1 Write each personal pronoun on a separate line. (**Remember: there are eight of them.**)

2 Against each one explain who or what it refers to.

To help you, here is the answer for the second one:
she: the writer's friend

Beautiful soup

I have a friend who makes Garbage Soup. Each week she clears out the vegetable rack and the fridge and boils and purees the lot with judicious additions. The result is delicious 'Garbage'. It is never the same twice, and it provides a good conversation piece as family and guests try to guess the contents. Liquidized soups have solid advantages. You can prepare them well in advance, they are cheap, and as you only need one pot and a spoon there isn't much washing up.

Earlier we saw that many personal pronouns have two forms:

I	me
we	us
she	her
he	him
they	them

The only ones that don't have two forms are:

you	you
it	it

We use the pronouns in the first column as the **subject** of the sentence and the ones in the second column the rest of the time:

- **I** don't like dogs.
- This dog came up to **me**.
- Then it bit **me**.

Exercise B

Choose the correct form of the pronoun in each of these sentences. Write it down.

1 If you ask (**I/me**) Maria isn't coming to school today.

2 (**She/Her**) wasn't on the bus this morning.

3 (**She/Her**) is sulking because Mr Tozer told (**she/her**) off yesterday.

4 (**He/Him**) shouted at Maria and (**I/me**) in maths.

5 (**He/Him**) was cross because (**he/him**) saw (**we/us**) whispering to each other.

More about objects

Exercise A

Read the following instructions. Some of the sentence objects have been missed out. They are listed on the right, together with other words and phrases that don't belong in the text. Write down the number of each space and the sentence object that should go in it.

Choose the sentence objects from this list:

a hat	*the bottle*	*them*
it	*the bowl*	*your arm*
me	*the cap*	*your grip*
more water	*the instructions*	
some pins	*the paper-clip*	

You will need:

- Plastic pen top with clip
- Plasticine
- Paper-clip
- Large plastic bottle with screw cap

Diver in a bottle

Follow __1__ to make this model diver. Then make __2__ float and sink by changing its density.

Make a plasticine figure 3.5 cm (1.25 in) long. Fix __3__ to its head and hang it from the pen top. Fill __4__ with water and drop in the diver.

The pen top should float with its top just above the water level. Make the figure bigger or smaller if needed. Then pour in __5__ and screw __6__ on tightly.

Squeeze the bottle to make the diver sink. Relax __7__ to make the diver rise.

Exercise B

In this part of the text, some sentence objects have been missed out. There is no list to help you. Think of a suitable object to fill each space.

Why the diver rises and sinks

When you put __1__ in the water, a bubble of air is trapped inside it. This trapped air bubble makes __2__ less dense than water, so it floats.

When you squeeze __3__, water squashes __4__ and takes up more space in the pen top. Now the diver is more dense than water, so it sinks.

When you relax __5__, the air in the pen top expands again. Now the diver is less dense than water, so it comes back up to the surface.

More experiments with objects

Exercise A

In the following text, some sentence objects have been missed out. Write down a suitable object to fill each space.

One-eye teaser

You use both your eyes to work out exactly where things are. This experiment shows __1__ why two eyes give you __2__ than one.

Close __3__ , then hold up __4__ in one hand and __5__ in the other, so they are level with your eyes.

With your arms slightly bent, try to put __6__ on the pen. Can you tell if the top is in front of the pen or behind it? Now try again using __7__ and see if it is easier.

Keep one eye tightly shut.

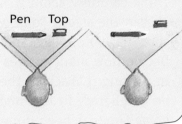

Pen   Top

Why you need two eyes

Two eyes give you two slightly different views. Your brain compares __8__ to work out exactly where things are.

When you close __9__ , you have only __10__ , so it is much harder for your brain to judge the distance between objects.

Exercise B

In this activity the instructions have been cut down to just a few words. Read them carefully and then write the instructions as complete sentences.

Make a tongue map

Did you know you use different parts of your tongue to taste things that are sour, salty, sweet and bitter? Draw a map of your tongue like the one here. Then try the tests below and fill in your results. (Some tastes are detected in more than one place.)

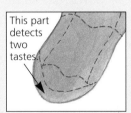

This part detects two tastes.

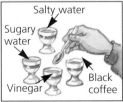

Salty water
Sugary water
Vinegar
Black coffee

Drinking straw dropper

Vinegar

Release finger.
Squeeze here.
Drop of liquid

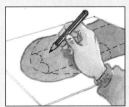

Instructions

four egg-cups
different tasting
   liquids
vinegar (sour)
salty water (salt)
sugary water (sweet)
black coffee (bitter)

two straws
  in half
droppers
dropper into vinegar
end
finger
hold liquid

drops of liquid
each area of tongue
  on map
dry tongue with bread
   between drops

note on map
taste vinegar strongly
rinse mouth
same test other tastes

Writing instructions

Now it's your turn to write some instructions. You are going to explain how to make something. You can:

- choose something that you already know how to do, or
- describe how to make the *steady hand game* which is illustrated on the next page.

Whichever you choose, you should write the instructions so that they can be understood by someone aged 8–10.

What to do

1 Decide what you are going to describe.

2 Think carefully about it. If you have chosen the *steady hand game* make sure that you understand it clearly.

3 Decide how many **stages** there are in making it. Each of these must be numbered. In the *steady hand game* this has been done for you.

4 For each stage,
- write the number
- list the main information you need to explain. Don't write complete sentences, just put down the main words.

5 When you have finished, look through what you have written and make sure you haven't missed anything out.

6 Now write the instructions stage by stage. Use your notes and write complete sentences.

7 When you have finished read through what you have written and ask yourself these questions:
- Have I given readers all the information they need at each stage?
- Have I taken anything for granted that I should explain?
- Have I missed out any stages?
Add any additional information that is needed.

8 Correct mistakes in:
- spelling
- punctuation
- grammar.

The steady hand game

You have probably played this game. It tests how steady and accurate your hand movements are. You have to get the wire loop from one end of the wiggly wire to the other without letting the loop touch the wire. If it does, a buzzer sounds and you have lost.

Materials

6-volt buzzer
4.5-volt battery
shoe box with top
1 m bendy wire without insulation

ballpoint pen
50 cm insulated wire
scissors
sticky tape

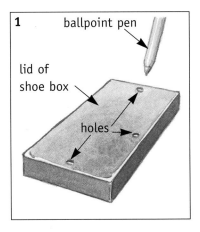

1
ballpoint pen
lid of shoe box
holes

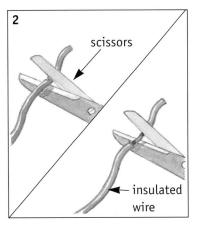

2
scissors
insulated wire

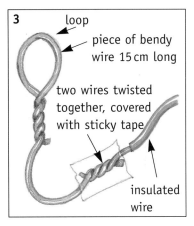

3
loop
piece of bendy wire 15 cm long
two wires twisted together, covered with sticky tape
insulated wire

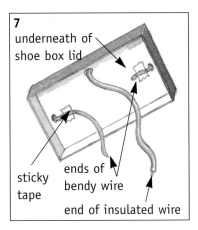

4
loop in bendy wire
insulated wire
shoe box lid

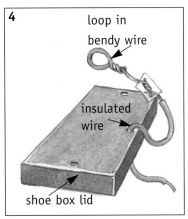

5
rest of the bendy wire bent into wiggly line

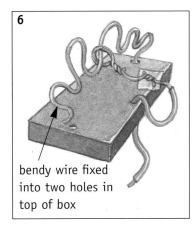

6
bendy wire fixed into two holes in top of box

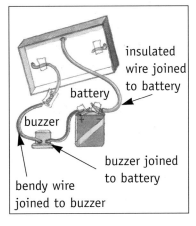

7
underneath of shoe box lid
sticky tape
ends of bendy wire
end of insulated wire

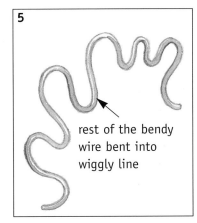

8
insulated wire joined to battery
battery
buzzer
bendy wire joined to buzzer
buzzer joined to battery

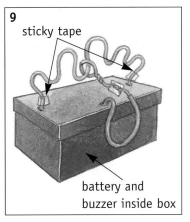

9
sticky tape
battery and buzzer inside box

Food, recipes and instructions

Why?

We can write about food for many different purposes:

- **to inform** – many books about food do this
- **to instruct** – recipes do this
- **to persuade** – some menus try to persuade us to eat the food at a restaurant or café.

Who?

We have to think very carefully about our readers:

- How much do they know?
- Are the instructions clear?
- Are the instructions in the right order?

Sentence objects

The object of a statement sentence:

- comes after the verb
- can be one word (a noun or pronoun), or a group of words
- refers to a different person or thing from the subject.

Exception: words ending in '-self' or '-selves' in sentences like this:
Eleanor cut herself on a piece of glass.

The object is often something that is affected in some way by the verb. The objects in the following sentences are underlined in **purple**:

Pam has just eaten my piece of cake. I wanted to eat it.

Pronouns

Personal pronouns have two forms:

Subject	Object and other uses
I	*me*
we	*us*
she	*her*
he	*him*
they	*them*

The only ones that don't have two forms are:

you	*you*
it	*it*

We use the pronouns in the first column as the **subject** of the sentence and the ones in the second column the rest of the time:

- **I** don't like dogs.
- This dog came up to **me**.
- Then it bit **me**.

Person and number

Pronouns can be **singular**:

   I   *she*

or **plural**:

   we   *they*

They are also described as being **1st**, **2nd** or **3rd** person. This is the full set:

	Singular	Plural
1st person	*I/me*	*we/us*
2nd person	*you*	*you*
3rd person	*he/him* *she/her* *it*	*they/them*

So 'I' is '1st person singular', 'we' is '1st person plural', and so on.

LISA goes on a school trip

In this unit we look at some of the places people go to on school trips.

- Which school trips can you remember most vividly?
- Which was the best and why?
- Was there a worst? If so, which one and why?
- They don't have 'holidays' on **LISA**'s planet. She wants to know what a holiday is. How would you explain the idea to her?
- Where would you take her to experience a 'typical holiday'?

In this unit you will learn about:

Describing and advertising:
- the different ways in which you can write about a place
- how we write for different purposes
- how we write for different audiences.

Noun phrases:
- how they are built up
- how they are used.

Possessives:
- using words like **my** and **mine**
- using apostrophe + s.

Writing a tourist leaflet:
- planning
- drafting
- editing and rewriting.

Country visits

LISA has been doing some research. These are some of the books and leaflets she has collected in preparation for her visit. Underneath there are short extracts from them. Look at them carefully, and then do the exercises on page 69.

A⬇ B➡

do the exercises on page 69.

Welcome to LAKE VYRNWY

Start your visit at:

Then explore the valley and enjoy:

The Visitor Centre - Where you will find the Severn Trent exhibition and the RSPB shop/information

Walking - short trails and long walks

Fishing - boat fishing for trout

Shopping - for local crafts and souvenirs

Lakeside Drive - with scenic lay-bys and information points

Refreshments - morning coffee, cream teas and gourmet meals

Water sports - canoes and sailing dinghies for hire.

C⬇

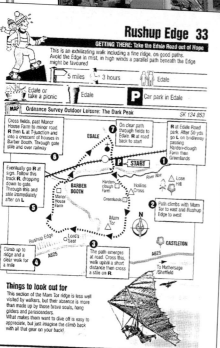

Rushup Edge 33

GETTING THERE: Take the Edale Road out of Hope

This is an exhilarating walk including a fine ridge, on good paths. Avoid the Edge in mist, in high winds a parallel path beneath the Edge might be favoured

5 miles | 3 hours | Edale

Edale or take a picnic | Edale | Car park in Edale

MAP Ordnance Survey Outdoor Leisure: The Dark Peak | SK 124 853

Cross fields, past Manor House Farm to minor road. **R** then **L** at T-junction and into a crescent of houses in Barber Booth. Through gate stile and over railway

On clear path through fields to Edale. **R** at road back to start

R at Edale Road park. After 50 yds go **L** on bridleway passing Harden-clough Farm then Greenlands

Eventually go **R** at sign. Follow this track **R**, dropping down to gate. Through this and stile immediately after on **L**

Climb up to ridge and a clear walk for a mile

The path emerges at road. Cross this, walk uphill a short distance then cross a stile on **R**.

Path climbs with Mam Tor to east and Rushup Edge to west

To Hathersage /Sheffield

CASTLETON

Things to look out for

This section of the Mam Tor ridge is less well visited by walkers, but their absence is more than made up by those brave souls, hang gliders and parascenders.

What makes them want to dive off is easy to appreciate, but just imagine the climb back with all that gear on your back!

33

SELF CATERING

Terms: Self Catering from £85-£285 per week | ♦♦♦♦ APPROVED

O. RUXTON MILL

Kings Caple **Contact: Milly Slater**

Set in beautiful Wye Valley, with lovely views. Spacious 3 bedroomed, converted cider mill and granary. Many exposed beams and stone work. Fishing available. Pets by arrangement.

Terms: Self Catering from £180 per week

♦♦♦♦ COMMENDED

P. THE ASHE

Bridstow **Contact: Thelma Green**

Spacious Granary Mill, Stable and Orchard Cottage. Sleeps 2-6, total of 18 people. Par 3 golf, tennis and fishing.

Terms: Self Catering from £100-£500 per week

♦♦♦♦ COMMENDED

Q. VAULD HOUSE FARM

The Vauld **Contact: Judith Wells**

Set amidst picturesque countryside, two spacious beautifully furnished cottages. Sleeps 5 + cot / 2 + cot this also ideal for the elderly or disabled. No smoking bedrooms. Pets by arrangement

D➡

HILL FARMING

FARMING

Hill farming takes place in all the main upland areas of Britain, especially in Scotland, Wales and parts of western Ireland. Smaller areas are found in the Pennines and Lake District, as well as Dartmoor and Exmoor in the south-west of Britain.

Conditions are often harsh in these areas and this makes farming difficult. Winters are cold and long, with snow covering the ground for several weeks. Rainfall is heavy, with up to 2,000 mm or more in a year, and the soils are generally shallow and infertile. Hill farmers do not grow many crops because conditions are not suitable, but they do rear animals, especially sheep. Dairy cattle are reared in the valleys near farm buildings, so that they can easily be brought in for milking. Beef cattle graze on the hillsides during the summer, but are brought nearer the farms in winter, when they are given other feed as well as grass.

Crofting is found mainly in the Hebrides, western Scotland and the Shetland Islands. In the past, crofts were made up of strips of common land which were divided amongst crofters every year. Now crofters have their own arable land fenced in, although they share common grazing land and farm

30

2

▲ Walking – short trails and long walks
▲ Birdwatching – from three hides round the lake
▲ Water sports – canoes and sailing dinghies for hire.

1

Ruxton Mill

Set in beautiful Wye Valley with lovely views. Spacious 3 bedroomed converted cider mill and granary. Many exposed beams and stone work. Fishing available. Pets by arrangement.

3 Conditions are often harsh in these areas and this makes farming difficult. Winters are cold and long, with snow covering the ground for several weeks. Rainfall is heavy, with up to 2,000 mm or more in a year.

4 Cross fields, past Manor House Farm to minor road. **R** then **L** at T-junction and into a crescent of houses in Barber Booth. Through gate stile and over railway.

Exercise A

1. The pictures on page 68 show four different publications. What are they? For each one, write down:
   a what it is called
   b the kind of information it gives
   c the kind of person who would use it.

2. Under the pictures there are four extracts, one from each publication. Write down the number of each extract and the letter of the publication it comes from.

Exercise B

1. Each of the four extracts contains clues that help us work out where it comes from. Write down the number of each extract and then explain what the clues are that tell us where it comes from.

2. Only Extract 3 is written in complete sentences. Why is each of the others written in a shorter form?

Seen from the air

This photograph was taken from a hot-air balloon. We can use it to illustrate many different kinds of writing.

Exercise C

The company that owns the hot-air balloon is producing a leaflet to advertise the flights. The company is going to use this picture in it. Write four or five sentences to go beside the photograph, telling people how interesting and exciting the trips are.

Exercise D

The picture is to go on the cover of a story book for children aged 7–9. The story is about a hot-air balloon trip. Write the first four or five sentences of the story.

Noun phrases

LISA asks:

You said in the last unit that the object of the sentence could be a single word or 'a group of words'. Earlier on you said the subject could be a single word or 'a group of words'. What is this 'group of words' you keep talking about?

A **phrase** is a group of words that work together as part of a sentence. A **noun phrase** can be the subject or the object of the sentence. It is built up on a noun or a pronoun. In these noun phrases the noun is printed in *italic* type:

Subject (noun phrase)	Rest of sentence
Chips	are revolting.
Those *chips*	are revolting.
Those soggy *chips*	are revolting.
Those cold soggy *chips*	are revolting.

Exercise A

In each of the following sentences, the subject is a noun phrase. Write it down and underline the noun it is based on.

Example
Sentence: *My new raincoat is green.*
Answer: My new <u>raincoat</u>

1. That fierce alsatian terrifies me.

2. Our new next door neighbours come from Halifax.

3. Only the largest computers can forecast weather accurately.

4. My 75-year-old grandmother is coming to stay.

Now do the same for the **objects** in these sentences:

5. Petra can't stand sickly sweet puddings.

6. Yesterday we had an unusual visitor.

7. Have you seen my red French book?

8. Those shoes cost a lot of money.

Exercise B

In each of the following sentences the subject or the object is a single noun. It is printed in bold type. Turn it into a noun phrase by adding at least two more words to it. Write out the whole sentence with the noun phrase underlined.

Example
Sentence: *Ice cream is delicious.*
Answer: <u>*This new raspberry-flavoured ice cream*</u> *is delicious.*

1. Don't tell me **stories**.

2. Emily likes painting **pictures**.

3. **Friends** came to see me in hospital.

4. I can't stand **cats**.

5. **Showers** are forecast for today.

6. Do you like **music**?

7. **Lessons** are boring.

8. Joanna likes reading **books**.

Being possessive

If you **possess** something, it belongs to you. You are the owner. In grammar we use the words **possessive** and **possession** to describe certain words and forms that show that something belongs to someone. Here are three examples:

That is *Peter's* book.　　This is *our* book.　　These books are *mine*.

Exercise A

LISA knows that **my** and **mine** are linked to **I** and **me**. Help her out by copying and completing this table:

I	me	my	mine
we			
you			
she	her		
he			
it		its	

Exercise B

Now **LISA** wants to know the difference between **my** and **mine**. She has collected the following sample sentences. Use them to explain the rule to **LISA**.

That is *my* coat.
That coat is *mine*.

Is that book *yours*?
Is this *your* book?

Give Diane *her* piece of cake.
Now give Sandra *hers*.

Exercise C

Apostrophe time!

In the examples that follow, the apostrophes are all in the right place:

- one girl's homework book
- many girls' homework books
- the children's homework books.

Explain in your own words what the rule is for putting an apostrophe when we want to show possession.

Exercise D

In each of the following sentences there are some words in brackets. Put the words in brackets into the correct form.

Example
Sentence: *That is (John book).*　　**Answer:** *John's book.*

1. Yesterday Sam broke her (father favourite chair).

2. I bought a card for my (parents wedding anniversary).

3. (The headteacher first school assembly) was really strange.

4. (Our old dog Rex kennel) is in a terrible state.

More about noun phrases

Exercise A

The passage below comes from a tourist leaflet. Some noun phrases have been missed out. They are listed in the wrong order after the passage. Write down the number of each space and the letter of the phrase you think should go in it.

___1___ stood on this site for 500 years. The Shrewsbury Quest is ___2___.

Enjoy creating ___3___ in the Scriptorium. Try your hand at the medieval art of calligraphy. Learn how the scribes made ___4___.

The hugely popular *Brother Cadfael* chronicles by Ellis Peters, now serialized on television, are set in the medieval Abbey at Shrewsbury, where ___5___ is the herbalist.

Phrases

A *a fascinating re-creation of medieval monastic life*

B *Brother Cadfael*

C *the Benedictine Abbey of St Peter and St Paul*

D *their inks and vellum*

E *your own decorated manuscript*

Exercise B

In this part of the same text, a number of noun phrases have been missed out. This time no help is given. Write down the number of each space and make up a suitable phrase to fit it.

Within the monastic gardens there is ___6___ dating from the 12th century. The only garden of its kind in England.

Solve the mystery ...

Dark deeds are afoot. Follow ___7___ and solve the Quest.

There are mysteries to solve for all ages and a regular prize draw. You can play ___8___ in the Cloisters or just sit and relax in the unique monastic gardens.

... Rest a while

Sample the fine Shropshire fare, inspired by medieval recipes and fresh local produce. It's ___9___.

Enjoy browsing in The Quest Shop, where you will find ___10___.

The holiday centre

Noun phrases are often used in adverts and leaflets that advertise things. You are going to write some advertising slogans for a new holiday centre. You are looking for short, snappy statements that tell people how good it is to visit. Look at the pictures and then follow the instructions at the bottom of the page.

The view

he accommodation

Exercise A

The first set of slogans is about the *view*. See how many different phrases you can make up about it. For example:

> *a stunning panoramic view*

Here are some words you could try:
amazing breathtaking sensational
extensive eye-catching fabulous
fantastic glorious magnificent
dazzling spectacular

Now try building up phrases on one of these key words:
vista   scenery   landscape

Exercise B

The next set of slogans describes the *accommodation*. Use one of these key words:
accommodation   apartments
flats   lifestyle

Some of these words may be useful:
attractive comfortable cosy
de luxe   inviting   luxurious
opulent   relaxing   spacious
well-appointed

Exercise C

Now make up a set of slogan phrases to describe the following *activities* that are on offer:

- sailing
- water-skiing
- canoeing
- karting
- crazy golf
- tennis.

Now is the time to use the writing skills you have been practising. You are going to write a tourist leaflet. Look at the leaflet below. This type of leaflet is designed to show people the attractions of a holiday place.

Severn Trent Water invite you to discover the magic of Lake Vyrnwy.

Not far away there's a secret valley that's waiting to welcome you. It's a land of rolling meadows, towering crags, raging waterfalls, mysterious forests, wild moorland – and one of Wales' largest and most beautiful lakes.

Come for the day, explore the valley and discover the magic of Lake Vyrnwy. Then stay for the night, in a choice of farmhouse B & B, self-catering cottages or a classic country hotel.

You'll find a warm welcome throughout the year. Visit Lake Vyrnwy soon, and enjoy a day that you'll never forget.

Created in the 1880s to supply Liverpool with water, Lake Vyrnwy and the surrounding countryside – 23,000 acres of forest, farms and moorland – are owned and managed by Severn Trent Water. Other organizations and the local community join in partnership with Severn Trent to ensure that this special area is well cared for.

Lead sentence
The leaflet begins with one sentence to catch the reader's eye. It tells us what the leaflet is about. It persuades us to read on.

The main text
Then there is a short description of the place and its attractions. Notice how it talks directly to the reader, as 'you'.

It tells us what the place is like, what we can do when we go there, and why we will enjoy it.

Extra information
At the end there is some extra information for people who might be interested – but you don't have to read it to get the main facts about the place.

Photographs
The leaflet has two photographs showing different aspects of the place. One shows the lake and one shows the countryside around it.

What to do

Choosing a subject

1 Decide the place you are going to advertise. It could be:

- ○ a local beauty spot
- ○ a local place of historical interest
- ○ somewhere you have visited on holiday
- ○ one of the places described on pages 72 and 73
- ○ somewhere you have made up.

Making some notes

2 Think about what you are going to write. Jot down ideas about these three topics:
a what the place looks like
b what people can do there
c why they will enjoy it.

Drafting sentences

3 Now think about topic (a): 'what the place looks like'. Write four or five sentences describing it as vividly as you can, building on the notes you have jotted down.

4 Do the same for topics (b) and (c).

Editing and rewriting

5 You should now have between twelve and fifteen sentences. For your leaflet you only need about half that number. Read through your sentences and think about how you are going to:

- ○ reduce the number of sentences
- ○ make your writing even more interesting and even clearer.

6 *For guidance on how to do this, look again at Exercise E on page 25.*

7 Rewrite your text so that it has between six and eight sentences.

Proof-reading

8 Now check your text for errors of:

- ○ punctuation
- ○ spelling
- ○ grammar.

Summing up what you've learned

Writing for different audiences and purposes

You can write about the same kind of topic for different audiences (**who**) and purposes (**why**). When we read we can get clues about this from the way the text is written:

- **the words that are used**
  Some texts want to persuade us how good something is. They use words like 'magnificent' and 'breathtaking'. Others are much more down-to-earth.
- **the way it is written**
  Some texts, like story books, use mostly complete sentences. Others use shorter forms (like phrases). Examples of this are instructions and leaflets.

Apostrophe + s

When we want to show that something belongs to someone or something we use an apostrophe. These are the rules:

1 Ask yourself, 'Who is the owner?'
2 After the last letter of the owner word, put in the apostrophe.
3 If the owner word doesn't end in one 's', add one 's' *after* the apostrophe.

Examples

Who is the owner?	What we write
Kelly	*Kelly's books*
the boys	*the boys' books*
the children	*the children's books*
James	*James' books*
the class	*the class's books*

Noun phrases

A **phrase** is a group of words that work together as part of a sentence. A **noun phrase** can be the subject or the object of the sentence. It is built up on a noun or a pronoun. In these noun phrases the noun is printed in *italic* type:

Subject (noun phrase)	Rest of sentence
Chips	are revolting.
Those *chips*	are revolting.
Those soggy *chips*	are revolting.
Those cold soggy *chips*	are revolting.

In these examples all the words have been added **before** the noun. You can also add them **after** it:
Those cold soggy *chips* on your plate ...
This is all one noun phrase.

Possessives

Earlier we looked at two different forms of the personal pronoun:

- **I** – the form we use for sentence subjects
- **me** – the form we use for objects and in other places in the sentence.

There are two others:

- **my** – the form we use with a noun, to show possession
- **mine** – the form we use on its own to show possession.

This gives us this set:

I	me	my	mine
we	us	our	ours
you	you	your	yours
she	her	her	hers
he	him	his	his
it	it	its	its

LISA tries to understand commercials

LISA has been watching TV and listening to the radio. She knows there are things called commercials, but she has some questions. Can you answer them for her?

- When TV started, there weren't any commercials. Why do we have them now?
- Do people enjoy watching them?
- Who are they for?
- Do they always tell the truth?

In this unit you will learn about:

Commercials:
- the language they use and why they use it
- who they are aimed at
- setting up your own advertising campaign.

Adjectives:
- how to change their meaning
- how to compare things using adjectives
- how to use them better.

Explaining commercials

They don't have advertising on **LISA's** planet, so she wants you to explain some commercials to her.

Exercise A

Look at the commercial on the right and then answer the questions below.

Questions

Answer these questions for **LISA:**

1. What is a film?

2. What is an All Day Breakfast?

3. What are BrekkyBurgerBars offering to give you?

4. What do you have to do to get it?

5. What does the commercial do to make it sound attractive?

6. Would it make you want to have a Kids' All Day Breakfast at BrekkyBurgerBars? What are your reasons?

Voice over

> Have you seen *Karrummbaah!*, the fun new film about those bouncy little creatures called Floppits? BrekkyBurgerBars have got some wonderful new Floppit toys just for you. There's a new one each week when you order a BrekkyBurgerBar Kids' All Day Breakfast.

Exercise B

1. The BrekkyBurgerBars commercial contains a number of words that have been chosen to make the film, the characters and the toys sound attractive. Write them down and explain why you think they have been chosen.

2. Think back to commercials you can remember. Make a list of other words that are popular with advertisers.

3. Choose two of them and explain why you think the advertisers like them.

A healthy life?

All the material on this page comes from a single packet of breakfast cereal. Who is it all for? And why?

Exercise A: The front

Look carefully at the front of the box. It is meant to attract our eyes and make us want to buy the product.

1 Who is it aimed at?

2 How does it try to attract them? Under the Kelloggs 'K' it says:

✓ Low in fat
✓ High in carbohydrates
✓ Rich in 3 B-vitamins
✓ Good source of iron

3 Who is this aimed at?

4 How does it try to attract them?

Exercise B: The back

The information below is taken from the back of the box. Read it and then answer these questions:

1 Look at the first four lines. Who do you think they are aimed at? Give reasons for your answer.

2 Now look at the rest of the information. Are these sentences aimed at the same audience as the rest of the text? What are your reasons for saying so?

Supercharged

Tony is calling everyone who loves the grrr-eat taste of Kellogg's FROSTIES

Beep…beep…beep…newsflash

Your favourite cereal has just been Supercharged to help you do your best. The one and only Supercharge formula gives you (per 30 g serving):

★ A load of carbohydrates that are a great fuel for your body as they are converted into energy more quickly and easily than fat.

★ Now half your daily needs (RDA) of three B-vitamins which help optimize the conversion of food into energy.

★ Three other essential B-vitamins that help produce healthy blood cells that carry the oxygen around your body.

★ Iron to help transport the oxygen to the cells in your body, including your muscles and brain.

Carbo-loaded, vitamin-packed Kellogg's FROSTIES – they're the Grrr-eatest!

Exercise C

1 What is your favourite breakfast food?

2 If you had to advertise it, which of these methods would you use and why:
- saying how good it is for you
- saying how good it tastes
- giving away free toys
- some other method (say what)?

It's really, really fast

My mum's car is fast.

My mum's c... is very fast.

My mum's car is fantastically fast.

My mum's c... is absolute... ultra **mega** fast. So the...

LISA has been listening to the way her friends use adjectives. Her computer needs more information about the words we use with adjectives to change their meanings.

Adjective phrases

Instead of using a single adjective, like 'fast', you can add to its meaning by putting one or more words before it:

- fast
- *very* fast
- *fantastically* fast
- *absolutely ultra mega* fast.

These words (*very, fantastically,* etc.) **modify** (change) the meaning of the adjective. The group of words is called an **adjective phrase**. You can use an adjective phrase wherever you use an adjective.

Exercise A

Each of the following sentences contains an adjective phrase. Write it down and underline the adjective.

1. That's a very nice bike you've got.
2. I'm feeling rather tired today.
3. Teresa is simply brilliant at maths.
4. What she said was a bit stupid.
5. She's bought a pretty expensive shirt.
6. The team's victory was slightly unexpected.
7. The geography test was so boring!
8. We had an absolutely wonderful holiday last year.
9. After the game the team felt completely gutted.
10. My brother got fairly good exam results.

Exercise B

1. Make a list of the words used to modify adjectives in Exercise A.
2. Write down five more words we can put in front of an adjective to change its meaning.

Exercise C

Look at the words you listed for Exercise B. Choose five of them and for each one explain how it changes the meaning of the adjective. Do it like this:

Phrase: *almost complete*
Word: *almost*
Answer: *It makes it less than complete.*

Comparing things ... and people

Comparative and superlative

When we compare things we sometimes use a different form
of the adjective. We add **-er** and **-est**:
high – higher – highest

For longer adjectives, we use **more** and **most** before the adjective:
interesting – more interesting – most interesting

We say that *higher* and *more interesting* are the **comparative**
forms of *high* and *interesting* – we are **comparing** them.

Highest and *most interesting* are the **superlative** forms.
'Superlative' means 'the most'.

Important

1 You can only **compare** *two* things or people.
2 You must have at least *three* to use the **superlative**:
   you can't have 'the best of two'.

Exercise A

In the text below there are a number of
blanks, each with an adjective in
brackets. Write down the number of the
blank and the correct word or words to
go in the spaces.

Example
Sentence: *Ravi is _____(clever) than
Dave, but Sarah is the
_____(intelligent) person
in the class.*

Answer: **cleverer, most intelligent**

Groovy stars ★ ★ ★ ★ ★

When it comes to funky film jobs, what
could be groovier than being a movie star?
Who wouldn't like the fame and the
admiration of thousands of fans – not to
mention a few million dollars thrown in?
Nowadays, Sylvester Stallone and Arnold
Schwarzenegger are some of the __1__
(famous) people in the world. These mega-
stars expect very special treatment, but there
was a time when things were very different.

For the first ten years of film making,
there were no stars at all. Cameras were the
__2__ (important) things on set and if there
were any signs of bad weather, the camera
was immediately sheltered, not the actors.

Horses were considered much __3__
(valuable) than human actors too, and were
__4__ (well) treated. After all, you could
always get another actor but trained horses
were much __5__ (hard) to find!

Stretch limousines are the __6__ (popular)
form of star travel, the general rule being
the __7__ (big) the car, the __8__ (big) the
star. Clark Gable had his car customized
so that it was exactly one foot __9__ (long)
than a rival's.

Using adjectives

We've already seen how useful adjectives can be – but there are so many of them. When you are writing you have to remember that:

- when you want to use an adjective, there is nearly always more than one to choose from, and
- you need to think carefully and pick exactly the right one.

Exercise A

Look at the following sentence:
The accident happened on a _____ day in January.

Any one of these adjectives could fill the gap:

bitter	*bleak*	*bracing*
chilly	*cold*	*cool*
freezing	*fresh*	*nippy*
parky	*sharp*	

But which one? Obviously it depends on what you want to say, but it helps if you have a clear idea of what they all mean. One way of doing this is to put them into a league table with the 'warmest' at the top and the coldest at the bottom, like the one on the right.

cool
freezing

1 Where would you put the other words in that league table?

2 The next set of words has been chosen to fill the gap in the following sentence:
It was raining and when I got home my clothes were _____.

Make up a league table for these words:

damp	*drenched*	*dripping*
moist	*soaked*	*sodden*
soggy	*sopping*	*waterlogged*
wet		

3 The final set of words has been chosen to fill the gap in the following sentence:
Dad was _____ when he heard what had happened.

Make up a league table for these words:

angry	*annoyed*	*cross*
displeased	*exasperated*	*furious*
irritated	*vexed*	

Exercise B

1 How many adjectives can you think of for hot weather? For example, there's 'warm' and 'sweltering'. Write down as many words as you can think of.

2 Make your list of adjectives into a league table.

Exercise C

Choose one of the league tables you have made up. Select three adjectives from it. Write three sentences, one for each adjective, showing the difference in their meanings.

Modifying adjectives

You learned on page 80 that you can put words in front of adjectives to change or **modify** their meaning. There are two groups of these **modifying** words. The following are the commonest:

Group A

amazingly   extremely   highly   incredibly
really   terribly   very

Group B

a bit   almost   fairly   quite
slightly

Exercise A

1 Each of the following sentences contains a word from Group A. Rewrite the sentence changing the Group A word for a word from Group B.

Example
Old sentence: *That sum was terribly difficult.*
New sentence: *That sum was a bit difficult.*

Try to use a different word each time.
a I'm very pleased with my new bike.
b That new teacher is extremely strict.
c When I saw Sam she was looking terribly unhappy.
d My dog gets really worked up when I take its bone away.
e This summer the weather has been incredibly hot.

2 Each of the following sentences contains a word from Group B. Rewrite the sentence changing the Group B word for a word from Group A.
a Our history lessons are fairly interesting.
b I keep my bedroom quite tidy.
c It's a bit cold today.
d The team were slightly surprised to win the match.

Exercise B

1 Look at the changes you made in the last exercise. Think about how they changed the meaning. Now answer this question: what is the difference between the two groups of words?

2 Which group would you put these words into?
rather   so   too

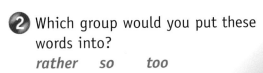

Advertising campaign

You have been asked to help advertise a new food product. You have to think up a set of slogans and to help design the new product pack.

Before you start

1 Decide what product you are going to advertise. You can choose a real food product, or one you have made up. It might be:
- a breakfast cereal
- a new kind of biscuit
- a new sweet
- a new chocolate bar.

2 If it is a made-up product, give it a name.

Slogans

3 Now you have to think up four advertising sentences to go in the spaces on the posters below. Three slogans should be about:
- how good the product is for you
- how good it tastes
- how new/exciting/different it is.

The fourth can be whatever you like. Make your sentences short and lively. Use the word bank on the next page to help you think of good sentences.

Designing the pack

Now you have to think about how you are going to make the pack so attractive that people will just *have* to buy it. In particular you have to decide what to put on the **front** and the **back** of the pack.

The front

On the front there is space for three things:

- the name of the product
- a picture
- one sentence.

4 Decide what picture you will have. It could be:

- the product itself
- the character you use to advertise the product
- something else you think people will find attractive.

Describe the picture you have chosen.

5 Think about the sentence you will use. It should not be one of the sentences you have used on your posters – but it could be based on them. Write it down.

The back

On the back there is space for about six sentences that explain exactly why the product is good to eat.

6 Decide who you are writing this for: who will read it?

7 Think about the main points you want to get across to them. Is it that:

- eating this is good for you
- eating it is fun
- only very special people eat this product
- or something else?

You could just concentrate on one of these or include them all.

8 Write your six sentences. Use the word bank below to help with ideas.

9 Look at what you have written and give your sentences a good heading.

Word bank

calorific	delectable	sweet	novel
easily digested	delicious	tasty	refreshing
healthy	finger-licking	breathtaking	sensational
high-calory	flavoursome	exceptional	special
low-calory	highly flavoured	exciting	uncommon
low-fat	moreish	exotic	unique
nourishing	mouth-watering	first	unusual
nutritious	oven-fresh	fresh	
protein-rich	scrumptious	individual	
slimming	spicy	latest	
appetizing	succulent	new	

Summing up what you've learned

The language of commercials

Commercials during children's TV are seen by:

- children
- their parents.

So they have to include:

- facts
- ideas
- language

suitable for these two different audiences.

The same is true of the packaging of breakfast cereals and other foods that children like. The children may like them but their parents have to pay for them!

Comparative and superlative

When we compare things we sometimes use a different form of the adjective:
high – higher – highest

Sometimes we use an extra word before the adjective:
interesting – more interesting – most interesting

We say that *higher* and *more interesting* are the **comparative** forms of *high* and *interesting* – we are **comparing** them. *Highest* and *most interesting* are the **superlative** forms.

Important

1 You can only **compare** *two* things or people.
2 You must have at least *three* to use the **superlative**: you can't have 'the best of two'.

Adjective phrases

Instead of using a single adjective, like 'fast', you can add to its meaning by putting one or more words before it:

- fast
- *very* fast
- *fantastically* fast
- *absolutely ultra mega* fast.

These words (*very*, *fantastically*, etc.) **modify** (change) the meaning of the adjective. The group of words is called an **adjective phrase**. You can use an adjective phrase wherever you can use an adjective.

Modifying words

There are two groups of words that we can use in this way:

- **words that add to the strength of the adjective**, like *very*, *terribly*, *really*
- **words that reduce the strength of the adjective**, like *fairly*, *slightly*, *a bit*.

-er/-est or more/most?

1 All one-syllable words add -er/-est.
2 Most words of more than one syllable use more/most.
3 Some two-syllable words add -er/-est:
    - words ending in 'y'
    - 'clever' and 'quiet'.
4 A few three-syllable words add -er/-est:
    - 'unhappy', 'unlucky'.
5 A small group of words can add -er/-est or use more/most:

common	cruel	gentle
narrow	pleasant	polite
shallow	simple	stupid

LISA gets into an argument

Of course no one ever has arguments on **LISA's** planet – they always agree and keep calm. **LISA** finds arguments like the one in the picture strange and interesting, but she can't really see the point.

- ◯ Why do people argue?
- ◯ Do you?
- ◯ Do you enjoy it?
- ◯ If you had to give **LISA** a definition of an argument what would you say?
- ◯ And is an argument different from these:
  row
  quarrel
  dispute?

In this unit you will learn about:

Facts, opinions and reasons:
- ◯ the difference between facts and opinions
- ◯ what happens when you give reasons for your opinions.

Sentence verbs:
- ◯ when the verb is a single word
- ◯ when the verb is a group of words
- ◯ what we mean by singular and plural
- ◯ how to make sure that the subject and the verb agree.

Story-telling:
- ◯ how to change from an 'I' story to a 'he/she' story.

Writing an argument

Fact or opinion?

When we speak or write, we can state facts or opinions.

- A **fact** is something you can prove to other people.
- An **opinion** is something you think or believe in but you can't prove to other people.

Facts

- Ben Nevis is the highest mountain in Great Britain.
- Paris is the capital of France.

Opinions

- Tottenham Hotspur are a great football team.
- Tea is better than coffee.

Exercise A

For each of the following statements, say if it is a fact or an opinion.

1. Kevin's new coat cost £125.
2. It's terrible.
3. He can afford it because he got £200 for Christmas from his Gran.
4. I wish I had a coat like that.
5. We've got a new maths teacher.
6. Her name is Mrs Graham.
7. Her lessons are much more interesting than Mr Green's.
8. She started algebra with us last week.
9. It's a bit confusing.
10. I got eight out of ten in the test yesterday.

Exercise B

Read the newspaper story on the right.

1. Find two statements of fact and write them down.

2. Find two expressions of opinion and write them down.

20-mile terror ride in runaway juggernaut

POLICE hailed a lorry driver as a hero today after he braved a 20-mile terror ride when his accelerator pedal suddenly stuck at high speed.

His ordeal began when he found he could not slow down as he drove south on the busy M1. The 25-year-old man from Potters Bar, Hertfordshire, alerted police on a mobile phone – while trying not to let the Scania lorry veer out of control as it thundered down the motorway at more than 70 m.p.h.

Five police cars and a helicopter were deployed to protect other motorists while the man, who has not been named, gave a running commentary of his predicament to a police operator.

'This must have been extremely terrifying for the man,' said a Hertfordshire police spokeswoman.

'But he managed to stay unbelievably calm and it is a credit to him that because of his actions and those of police officers, neither he nor any other motorists were hurt.'

Opinions and reasons

Everyone has opinions. Some people have opinions for no real reason.
Other people can give good reasons for their opinions.

Exercise A

Read the conversation below and then answer the questions that follow it.

KAREN: *I don't eat chips.*

GARY: *Don't eat chips? Everyone eats chips!*

KAREN: *My Mum says they're bad for me. Too much fat and starch.*

GARY: *'Too much fat and starch.' Your Mum must be crazy. Chips are great, and what's that cakky stuff in the bottom of your lunch box?*

KAREN: *Lentils.*

GARY: *Ugh, gross! Looks like dog sick.*

DEBBIE: *Shut up, Gary, you're putting me off my dinner.*

GARY: *Well, she's putting me off mine. Look at that muck in her lunch box. Is her Mum a health freak, or what?*

KAREN: *She's not a freak but she doesn't let me eat rubbish like you eat.*

GARY: *This is lovely grub. What do you mean?*

KAREN: *We're vegetarians.*

GARY: *Don't eat meat? You don't know what you're missing.*

RINA: *It's what you're used to, Gary. We don't eat meat either.*

KAREN: *We shouldn't be killing animals just so we can eat them. What about all those poor calves chained up in crates for the whole of their lives? It's cruel.*

GARY: *They're only animals. They can't feel anything.*

1 Find two opinions that the speaker doesn't give any reasons for.
Write the opinions down.

2 Find one speaker who does give a reason for their opinion.
Write down the opinion and the reason for it.

3 What do you think about this subject? Write a sentence expressing your opinion and another sentence explaining the reasons for it.

The verb phrase

Exercise A: Revision

How much can you remember about verbs? **LISA** tested her computer to make sure that it had recorded the information about verbs. What it came up with is shown on the right. Unfortunately it has missed some key words. Write down the number of each blank and the word that should go in it.

Definition of a verb

A verb is a part of a ___1___.
In a statement sentence it normally comes ___2___ the subject.
We use verbs to describe ___3___.
We also use them to describe ___4___ and states of mind.
The verb in a sentence can be ___5___ ___6___ or a group of words.

When the verb is more than one word

So far, all the verbs you have looked at have been just one word, but a lot of the time, the verb is made up of a group of words – a **phrase**. In the following sentences, the **verb phrase** is printed in red:

> *That car is travelling too fast.*
> *It will crash.*
> *They were saving up for a holiday.*
> *They have visited Italy before.*

Exercise B

Write down the verb in each of the following sentences. In some of them the verb is just one word, in some it is a group of words.

1. Gemma is having problems with algebra.
2. Yesterday she was doing her homework in tears.
3. Her mother had been good at maths at school.
4. She decided to help her.
5. She looked carefully at all the problems.
6. She tried to explain them to Gemma.
7. Gemma just got more confused.
8. In the end they had an argument.
9. Gemma's mother went off in a temper.
10. Gemma had to do the problems on her own.

Do they agree?

LISA has noticed that sometimes you have to change the verb a bit if you change the subject. We say:

*Siobhan **likes** geography.*

but:

*Siobhan and Gemma **like** French.*

When do we say 'like' and when do we say 'likes'?

Exercise A

1 Copy and complete the table on the right.

2 Now explain to **LISA** the rules for when we use **like** and when we use **likes**.

3 Now make similar tables for each of the following:
am – is – are
was – were
do – does

I	like	we	___
you	___		
he	___	they	___
she	___		
it	___		

Exercise B

Sometimes it is difficult to know which form of the verb to use. Look at the following sentence. Which form of the verb is correct?

All my friends except Peter – support/supports – Luton Town FC.

The way to work it out is to ask yourself, 'Which pronoun could I use to replace the subject?' Here the answer is 'they'. So the verb should be 'support'.

For each of the sentences on the right, write down the correct form of the verb.

1 All the teachers for Year 7, including Mr Lambert, – is/are – easy to understand.

2 All the people on this school trip, except for that idiot Mark James, – has/have – behaved really well.

3 Either Siobhan or Gemma – is/are – late for the bus every day.

4 Both David and Patrick – has/have – been in trouble at school recently.

5 The staff at our school – is/are – usually quite friendly.

Using verb phrases

Exercise A

In the story on the right, some of the verbs have been missed out and replaced by a blank. In the middle of the blank you will see a number and the verb in brackets. Write down the number of the blank and the correct form of the verb. (You may have to add words like **was**.)

Example

As he ___1 (go)___ along the road he saw the car.

Answer

1 was going

The pigeons flew out of the alley in one long swoop and ___1 (settle)___ on the awning of the grocery store. A dog ___2 (run)___ out of the alley with a torn Cracker Jack box in his mouth. Then came the boy.

The boy ___3 (run)___ hard and fast. He stopped at the sidewalk, looked both ways, saw that the street was deserted and kept going. The dog ___4 (catch)___ the boy's fear, and he started running with him.

The two of them ran together for a block. The dog's legs were so short he appeared to be on wheels. His Cracker Jack box ___5 (hit)___ the sidewalk. He kept glancing at the boy because he ___6 (not know)___ why they were running. The boy ___7 (know)___. He did not even notice the dog beside him or the trail of spilled Cracker Jacks behind.

Exercise B

In the part of the story on the right here, some verbs have been missed out. They are listed below, but they are not in the correct form. (They aren't in the right order, either.) Write the number of each blank and the correct form of the verb that should go in it.

Verbs

chase	not stop
go	see
not answer	sit

The boy talks to his mother

'Sit down. Tell me what's wrong.' He hesitated and then sat beside her on the sofa. She waited and then said again, 'What's wrong?'

He ___1___ for a moment. He looked out of the window, and he could see the apartment across the street. A yellow cat ___2___ in the window watching the pigeons. He said in a low voice, 'Some boys ___3___ to kill me.'

'Not *kill* you, Benjie,' she said. 'No one is – '

He glanced quickly at her. 'Well, how do I know what they're going to do?' he said, suddenly angry. 'They ___4___ me, that's all I know. When you ___5___ somebody chasing you, and when it's Marv Hammerman and Tony Lionni and a boy in a black sweat shirt you ___6___ and say, "Now, what *exactly* are you guys planning to do – kill me or just break a few arms and legs"?'

Who's telling this story?

Sometimes it's best to tell stories as 'I' – in the first person singular. Other stories are better if you use the third person: 'he' or 'she'. One famous writer says it's a good thing to try writing as 'I' and then changing the story round to a 'he/she' story.

Exercise A

Below is part of a story told in the first person. If we rewrite it in the third person, the first sentence becomes, 'He wanted a mouth-organ, he wanted it more than anything else in the whole world.'

Rewrite all the sentences that would need changing. If a sentence doesn't need changing, don't write it down.

I wanted a mouth-organ, I wanted it more than anything else in the whole world. I told my mother, she kept ignoring me but I still wanted a mouth-organ badly.

I was only a boy. I didn't have a proper job. Going to school was like a job, but nobody paid me to go to school. Again I had to say to my mother, 'Mum, will you please buy a mouth-organ for me?'

It was the first time now that my mother stood and answered me properly. Yet listen to what my mother said. 'What d'you want a mouth-organ for?'

'All the other boys have a mouth-organ, mam,' I told her.

'Why is that so important? You don't have to have something just because others have it.'

'They won't have me with them without a mouth-organ, mam,' I said.

'They'll soon change their minds, Delroy.'

'They won't, mam. They really won't. You don't know Wildo Harris. He never changes his mind. And he never lets any other boy change his mind either.'

'Delroy, I haven't got the time to argue with you. There's no money to buy a mouth-organ. I bought you new shoes and clothes for Independence Celebrations. Remember?'

'Yes, mam.'

'Well, money doesn't come on trees.'

'No, mam.' I had to agree.

'It's school-day. The sun won't stand still for you. Go and feed the fowls. Afterwards milk the goat. Then get yourself ready for school.'

She sent me off. I had to go and do my morning jobs.

Exercise B

Now it's time to try this on one of your own stories.

1 Find a story you have already written in the first person.

2 Take the first page and write it again as a third person story.

3 When you have finished, read both versions and answer this question: which is better to read, and why?

What I think is ...

Exercise A

In the script on page 89 you read about different opinions about food. Read the script again and then the real-life interview below. Then answer the question on the right:

1 Who do you think puts forward the best argument: Gary or Karen on page 89, or Clare on this page? What are your reasons? What is your opinion about vegetarianism? What are your reasons for your opinion?

INTERVIEWER: *Clare, you're a vegetarian. Tell us about that.*

CLARE: *Well, I just don't agree with the way they are killed, the way they are kept. So I thought, 'No, I can't put up with this any more, so I'll just eat vegetables.' I mean I'd rather go out – say with a gun – and kill a pigeon myself, take it home, pluck it, skin it, cook it. I'd rather do that than go to a supermarket and buy this dead bird that's on display.*

INTERVIEWER: *But you actually like meat?*

CLARE: *Yes – I love it! But I prefer to see it live and being well treated or free or something – as opposed to being stuck in a little box.*

INTERVIEWER: *You're a vegetarian, but do you eat eggs and milk?*

CLARE: *I eat free-range eggs, yes, and I drink milk.*

Exercise B

On the right there are outlines of three topics people often argue about.

1 Choose one of them.

2 Write one or two sentences saying what your opinion is about this topic.

3 Write one or two sentences explaining your reasons.

4 Now do the same for the other two topics.

Huntin', shootin', fishin'
A lot of people think that fox hunting and deer hunting should be banned. But what about shooting pheasants, hares and rabbits? And should angling be banned, too?

A sporting nation?
British teams are not as successful as people would like. What is the answer: more sport at school? better sports facilities ...?

Private cars – public transport
Private cars cause pollution. Campaigners say we must use cars less to save the planet and use public transport instead. What do you think?

What I say is ...

Now you are going to work on building up one argument in detail.

Exercise A

1 Choose one of the topics you thought about for Exercises A and B on page 94.

2 Look at what you wrote before.

3 Now take a piece of paper and rule it out like this:

What I think: _____	
Reasons for my opinion	*Reasons against my opinion*

4 After '*What I think*', write down your opinion. For example, you could write:
What I think: that all forms of hunting, shooting and fishing should be banned.

5 Now think of as many reasons as you can to explain *why* you hold that opinion. Write them all in the '*for*' column.

6 Some people don't agree with you. Think about the reasons they give for disagreeing. Write them in the '*against*' column.

Exercise B

Now it is time to write out your argument. Write the following sentences:
- one sentence stating your opinion
- three or four sentences explaining why you think that
- two or three sentences explaining the reasons why people might disagree with you
- two or three reasons explaining why you think they are wrong and you are right.

You may find it helpful to look at the word bank on the right to find words and phrases you can use in your sentences.

Word bank	
agree	disagree
explain	persuade
reason	argument
proof	case
statement	evidence
but	therefore
because	as
since	so
on the one hand	on the other hand
in favour of	opposed to

Summing up what you've learned

Facts, opinions and reasons

When you make a statement it may be a fact or an opinion.

Facts

Facts are statements you can **prove** beyond doubt – or that everyone agrees with anyway. For example:

My dad is 35 years old.

Opinions

Opinions are statements that are not easy to prove beyond doubt. They tell people about what you **think** or **believe**. For example:

'EastEnders' is a load of rubbish.

Reasons

When we express our opinions we sometimes try to explain them by giving **reasons**. We may use these reasons to persuade other people that our opinion is right:

It's very important to get good marks in maths at GCSE. **Then you can get a better job.**

Verb phrases

The verb in a sentence can be a single word or a group of words – a **phrase**. In the following sentences, the verb is printed in red:

The car was travelling too fast. It crashed.

Agreement

We saw in **Unit Six** that pronouns can be **singular** or **plural**, and **1st**, **2nd** or **3rd person**:

	Singular	Plural
1st person	I	we
2nd person	you	you
3rd person	he	they
	she	
	it	

The verb changes to **agree** with the subject:

I	walk	am	have
you	walk	are	have
she/he/it	walks	is	has
we	walk	are	have
they	walk	are	have

Writing an argument

Sometimes you will be asked to explain what you think about a topic and to give your reasons. If you are going to do this well you need to do the following things:

Thinking

1 Know what you think.
2 Make a list of the reasons why you think that.
3 Think of reasons people might have for disagreeing with you.
4 Know why you think people who disagree are wrong.

Writing

5 Make a plan (a list of the main things you want to say in the right order).
6 Write the argument. Make sure that you include points 1-4 on the left.

Problems with the computer

Sometimes **LISA's** on-board computer causes her all sorts of difficulties. In this unit you will have to give her a lot of help with her language problems.

In this unit you will revise:

The what, who, why, where and how of writing
Directive sentences
Sentence objects
Pronouns
Noun phrases
Apostrophes
Possessives
Adjectives
Adjective phrases
Verb phrases
Facts, opinions and reasons

LISA looks at language

LISA's computer analyses language all the time. It has invented a way of sorting it all out by asking five simple questions.

What?

We talk and write about many different subjects during a day. There are special words for different subjects. The computer can work out the subject from the special words used.

Why?

We write and talk for many different purposes and this shows in the words and sentences we use. Here are some common purposes:

- **to inform**
  For example, the main purpose of encyclopaedias is to provide information.

- **to instruct**
  School rules and cookery recipes both tell us what to do.

- **to persuade**
  TV commercials, for example, set out to persuade us to buy something – they want to change the way we think about things.

- **to entertain**
  Stories and TV soaps are both meant to entertain – they are for our enjoyment.

Who?

We write and talk differently for different people. (Think about the difference between how you talk to your close friends and how you talk to the headteacher!) **LISA** is interested in this – on her planet everyone speaks in exactly the same way to everyone else.

Where?

LISA's computer is also making a record of where each of the messages it records has come from: everywhere from encyclopaedias to graffiti!

How?

LISA's computer has worked out that there are four main kinds of writing people do:

- stories
- descriptions
- explanations
- opinions and arguments.

Exercise A

On this page there are some of the examples the computer has collected. Each one is followed by two questions. Your job is to read the extract and then answer the questions. Here is an example to help you:

Text

Set oven at 375°F or Mark 5. Sift the flour and 3½ oz caster sugar three times and set on one side. Place the egg whites, salt and cream of tartar in a large, dry basin and whisk with a rotary beater until foamy. Add the remaining sugar, 2 tablespoons at a time.

Answer

Why?

To instruct people how to cook something.

Where?

From a magazine about food, or a cookery book.

Questions: Why? Where?

1

Mr White's classroom was immaculate. The tables and chairs, which looked new, were evenly spaced and facing the front. Every book, every folder was stacked neatly. Nothing was out of place.

Questions: What? How?

2

Two teenagers baffled Cotswold villagers when they tried to set the world to rights by painting a red telephone box blue.

At Cheltenham magistrates' court yesterday, solicitor David Billingham explained why Paul Usher, aged 19, of Longlands Road, Bishops Cleeve, and a 17-year-old caused £572 worth of damage to the box in Bishops Cleeve.

Questions: Where? How?

3

Most people have about 100,000 hairs on their heads. Fair-haired people can have 150,000 and red-haired people have to make do with about 90,00. Hair grows at about 1 cm a month or 0.33 mm a day. Hot weather makes your hair grow faster.

Questions: Why? How?

4

1 Remove cartridge from bag.

2 Fill jug with tap water and submerge cartridge in water. Agitate cartridge to remove all bubbles.

3 Place cartridge in hopper pushing firmly and evenly into position.

Questions: Where? How?

Directives, objects and pronouns

Exercise A

LISA has been having another look at **directive sentences**. Can you tell her which of the following sentences is a directive?

1. Making scrambled egg is easy.
2. First get two eggs.
3. You will also need salt, butter and milk.
4. Crack the eggs into a basin.
5. Beat them up with a little salt and 1 tablespoonful of milk.

She needs some more examples. Make up five more directive sentences for her, using the following verbs:

○ mix   ○ heat   ○ melt   ○ serve   ○ stir.

Exercise B

LISA has also been having another look at **sentence objects**. She wants to know the objects in the following sentences. Some are one word and some are a group of words.

1. You will need all the ingredients in the list.
2. Beat the butter and the sugar together.
3. Add the spices.
4. Mix in the flour.
5. Crack one egg into a bowl.
6. Beat it into the mixture.
7. Roll this dough into a ball.
8. Wrap it in clingfilm.
9. You should store it in the fridge for about an hour.
10. Roll the dough out with a rolling pin.

Exercise C

LISA has had some difficulties with **personal pronouns**. In the following extract there are several blanks with two pronouns in brackets. Can you tell her:

a which one is correct
b the reason why?

Jenny and Sam had a problem about their mother's birthday. They wanted to buy ___1 (she/her)___ a birthday present. Unfortunately for ___2 (they/them)___ , ___3 (they/them)___ didn't have enough money. Jenny only had 15p and Sam had even less than ___4 (she/her)___ . ___5 (She/Her)___ had just 12p.

Can you tell her the rule? Explain when we use **she** and **they** and when we use **her** and **them**.

Noun phrases and possessives

Exercise A

In each of the following sentences the subject or the object is a single noun. It is printed in bold type. Turn it into a **noun phrase** by adding *at least two* more words to it. Write out the whole sentence with the noun phrase underlined.

Example
Sentence: *Ice cream is delicious.*
Answer: *This new raspberry-flavoured ice cream is delicious.*

1 **Films** are more fun than books.

2 **People** find my accent funny.

3 **Sunshine** can be bad for you.

4 My mother can't stand **dogs**.

5 **Visitors** like going to EuroDisney.

6 Do you like **meat**?

Exercise B

In each of the following sentences there are some words in brackets.
Put the words in brackets into the correct form.

Example
Sentence: *That is (John book).*
Answer: *John's book.*

1 (Our new English teacher lessons) are really interesting.

2 Peter has played in all (the first team last six games).

3 That song is (all my friends favourite).

4 I've lost (James pen).

5 Fashions in (women clothes) change very fast.

How do we use an **apostrophe** to show possession? Write a short explanation.

Exercise C

LISA still hasn't quite got the hang of **possessives**. Help her by choosing the correct form for each of the following sentences:

1 I have lost (my/mine) pen.

2 That pen is (my/mine).

3 Have you got (your/yours) book?

4 Is this book (your/yours)?

Now help her with the rules:

5 Make a list of *all* the possessives.

6 Explain when and how they are used.

Adjectives and adjective phrases

Exercise A

LISA is still collecting **adjectives**. She has found the following sentences about the human body. After each sentence the number in brackets tells you how many adjectives it contains. Write down the adjectives in each sentence.

1 Your blood is yellow! (1)

2 If you leave a test tube full of blood for some hours, the blood cells sink to the bottom and you're left with a clear yellow fluid. (3)

3 The yellow stuff is called plasma – it's 90 per cent water and 10 per cent chemicals, such as those tasty molecules and minerals that your cells need to grow and stay healthy. (3)

Exercise B

LISA's also collecting **adjective phrases**.

1 Find two adjective phrases in the following extract and write them down:

When red blood cells take oxygen from the lungs they're bright red. But after the cells give up their oxygen they're dark red. This is why you get dark red blood in veins returning to the heart.

2 Find one adjective phrase in the following sentence and write it down:

Your heart is strong enough to pump blood round your body in one minute.

Exercise C

Copy and complete the following table:

Adjective	Comparative	Superlative
big	bigger	biggest
beautiful	more beautiful	most beautiful
easy		
remarkable		
bad		
sharp		
unusual		
angry		
extraordinary		
rapid		
careful		
famous		

Verb phrases

Exercise A

Just testing ... Write down the **verbs** in each of the following sentences:

1 Androids are machines that look and behave like human beings.

2 Instead of a heart and a brain they have a computer.

3 A group of these creatures has been sent from Planet K48Z46.

4 They are going to investigate our life and language.

5 **LISA** is the Language Investigation Specialist Android.

6 She has got the job of learning English.

7 Then she will teach it to scientists on K48Z46.

8 Sometimes **LISA's** computer goes wrong.

9 This can cause terrible problems.

10 Still, **LISA** is enjoying her stay on earth.

Exercise B

The verbs in the following sentences are missing. There is a list of verbs below but not all the verbs in the list come from the passage. Write down the number of each blank in the sentences. Against it write the missing verb – make sure it is in the correct form.

The sun ___1___ over the walled city of Syracuse. It ___2___ the end of one of the hottest days of the year. On top of the city walls the guards ___3___ up and down nervously. Far below them in the harbour, the enemy ships ___4___ gently. The Romans. There ___5___ a few lights showing on the ships, cooking fires and torches, but not much movement. The Romans (not) 6 ___ tonight. The guards ___7___ their sweating brows and ___8___ on their spears. The city itself was lit and the sky was bright with stars, but the path below the walls was in deep shadow. Even if the guards ___9___ over the walls and peered down, they wouldn't have seen the small door open at the foot of the tower. They ___(not) 10___ the man in the dark cloak step out and close the door quietly behind him.

Verbs

attack	be	hope	pace	rock	see	wipe
be	expect	lean	rest	run	set	wonder

LISA reports to K48Z46

LISA has to make regular reports back to her planet. She has decided that she should send some of them in English – for practice.

Exercise A

One of LISA's early messages is shown below. In it, she missed out all the punctuation. Correct her message by writing it out with the correct punctuation.

a group of the humans from class 7r took me to bennys brilliant burger bar bennys is a place where they go to take on fuel this fuels very strange they kill animals and mince their flesh they mix this with vegetables called onions and make it into little flat cakes then they heat it up very hot its called frying they put the little cake inside a round cake of bread and put coloured liquids called relishes on it then they eat it this means that they put pieces of it into their mouths and take them down inside their bodies

Exercise B

In the next message LISA got very confused about pronouns. Correct her message by writing it out with the correct pronouns.

These young humans are taught how to make its own fuel — or food as he call it. Me watched they having a lesson at them's school. The teacher began by telling they that it was going to show they how to make something called spaghetti Bolognaise. This is a very popular food in England. It cut up an onion and fried her. Then your added some meat and some tomato. Then us mixed this up together and cooked she to make a sauce. Its left this to keep hot while it cooked the spaghetti. This is long white rods which are put into boiling water and cooked until we are soft and slimy. Then the hot sauce is poured over you. These humans are very strange!

Exercise C

In her third message **LISA** wanted to use some adjective phrases.
Unfortunately she didn't get them quite right. Write down the adjective phrases
she has used and suggest a better version for each one.

Sometimes the young humans are taken travelling by their teachers. The
first journey I went on with them was to a lake in Wales. We travelled in
a coach and the journey was almost long. By the time we arrived, some
of the children were half tired, but when they saw the lake they got
partly excited. The lake was well large and we stopped at the visitors'
centre. Here there is an altogether interesting display about the lake. The
children had to go round and make totally careful notes. After that their
teachers sent them for a nearly short walk along the shore of the lake.
They had to look for interesting plants. One of them came back with an
entirely enormous flower. She said it came from the lake shore but her
teachers were dearly certain that she had taken it from the garden of a
house near the lake.

Exercise D

In the fourth message **LISA's** computer forgot how to make correct verb
phrases. Write out the incorrect verb phrases she has used. Against each one
write what it should have been.

At the end of the summer term the children from Class 7R was gone to
London. They am travelling in a train to Paddington Station. When they
have got there they will travel on another train which are going
underground. Some of the children was being quite frightened because
they never gone on an underground train before. The train have been
taking them to Piccadilly Circus station. Then they all will be going up a
moving staircase and out into the open air again. Piccadilly Circus had
been a large roundabout with a statue in the centre. The children be taken
along the street to a large square which would be called Trafalgar Square.
It might be having a column in the centre on top of which there should
have been a statue of Lord Nelson. All around people will feed the pigeons
that had lived in this place.

Oh yes it was ... Oh no it wasn't!

Exercise A

LISA's on-board computer has recorded the conversation between the two drivers in the picture above. They are arguing about:

- what happened
- whose fault it was.

1 Write down what you think they said to each other.

2 Write it as a script.

3 Call the drivers 'A' and 'B'.

4 Write between ten and fifteen sentences.

5 Make sure that your script is correctly set out and punctuated. Make sure it contains facts, opinions and reasons.

Exercise B

Now read through what you have written in Exercise A.

1 Find one sentence that states a **fact**. Write it down.

2 Find two sentences that express an **opinion**. Write them down.

3 Find one sentence that contains a **reason** for an opinion. Write it down.

I want you to think back to the very first thing you can remember in your life ...

Remembering the past

- ● What is the very first thing that you can remember from your own life?
- ● What details of it can you remember?
- ● What problems do you think **LISA** might have in answering the question the teacher in the picture asks?
- ● What do you think she might say?

In this unit you will learn about:

Past and future:
- ● different kinds of writing about the past and the future:
  - – who it is for
  - – why it was written
  - – how we know
- ● sorting out what is past, present and future
- ● working out the order of events in a story.

Diaries and plans:
- ● how we write when writing diaries about the past and describing plans for the future.

Autobiography:
- ● planning and writing about our own lives, past and future.

Looking back

LISA has been reading about the past. The texts she
has collected are shown below.

1

20 December
Frost and snow. Ted and I nearly
lost our fingers pulling snow-
frozen ivy off the trees to decorate
the cottage. The car broke down.

2

The bruised Brits had been battered for a
thousand years. In 43 AD the Romans
ruined them, in the 5th century Saxons
savaged them, in the 9th century the
Vikings vanquished them. These were the
Dark Ages. (No jokes about them being
called 'Dark' because there were a lot of
'knights' around in those days.)

But in 1066 the Normans finally
nobbled them.

3

His BMW had reeled off a smooth 1,500
miles to Scotland and back before
Graham McCalliom realised he had a
whisker of trouble under the bonnet.

Inside, a rather miserable looking cat
was wedged in next to the radiator.

The well travelled tabby is thought
to have been stuck there for two days,
joining Mr McCalliom, a wedding
photographer from Wootton Bassett,
Wiltshire, on his journey to Edinburgh,
Glasgow, Ayr, London and back
to Swindon.

He was visiting friends there when
he spotted a long tail hanging from the
bottom of his J-reg 5-series BMW.

'It started moving,' he said. 'I
couldn't believe it.'

4

Having waited many weeks to cross the
Channel, the Normans attacked the
Anglo-Saxon army waiting at Hastings.
Harold of England, having been given
the time to return from the north, where
he had defeated his other rival, Harold
of Norway, was confident of further
success. But on 28 September he died
in battle, pierced through the eye by
a Norman arrow. William, now the
Conqueror, was crowned in Westminster
Abbey at Christmas.

Exercise A

LISA needs some help in working out **what kind of writing** each of the texts
above is. Look carefully at each one and then answer the following questions:

1 Where does it come from?

2 What makes you think so?

3 What kind of person do you think it was written for?

4 What makes you think so?

Looking ahead

Now **LISA** has been reading about the future. On this page are the texts she has collected. They are all from newspapers. For each exercise read the text and then answer the questions.

Exercise A

England, Wales and Northern Ireland will be cloudy with outbreaks of rain, heavy at times, though there will be sleet or snow for a time over northern England, especially over hills. It will become mild and windy in the south but will remain cold in the north.

1 Which part of the newspaper does this come from?

2 How do you know this?

3 What kind of reader would be interested in this extract?

Exercise B

If you're at a loss as to what to do in your career then after today you'll have a greater idea of what it is you want to do. By following your intuition you'll find yourself following a path that is right up your street. A fantasy may become reality now.

You'll hear from someone you'd lost touch with and the reunion will be better than you could ever envisage.

4 What part of the newspaper does this come from?

5 How do you know this?

6 There are two blanks in this extract. What do you think might go in them?

7 What kind of reader would be interested in this extract?

Exercise C

Beach team goes on patrol

A new team of wardens is to begin patrolling Weston-super-Mare's golden sands and parks to keep the popular sites trouble-free.

Resort bosses say the Ranger Service, which gets under way this summer, will put a stop to the problems posed by vandals, illegal traders and speeding boy racers.

And they are confident that reinstating patrols in parks and gardens, which were axed in 1993 due to budget cutbacks, will encourage people to make more use of them.

Three full-time and two part-time rangers are to be recruited and will monitor activities on the seafront, parks and open spaces throughout the town.

8 This extract comes from the news section. Which parts tell us about things that have already happened?

9 What does the rest of it tell us about?

10 What kind of reader would be interested in this extract?

Exercise A

On **LISA's** planet, the creatures don't talk about **past**, **present** and **future**. They just talk about *now* and *not now*. So **LISA** finds our ideas difficult to understand. Can you write short explanations of the meanings of 'past', 'present' and 'future' to help her out?

Exercise B

For each of the following sentences:

a say whether it is about the past, the present, or the future

b explain which word or words tell(s) you this.

1. The bruised Brits had been battered for a thousand years.

2. It will become mild and windy in the south.

3. You'll hear from an old friend.

4. The car broke down.

5. He spotted a long tail hanging from the bottom of his car.

6. I'm going to get even with her.

7. You are at your friskiest today.

8. On 28 September he died in battle.

9. This is not a day to be shy.

10. In 1066 the Normans finally nobbled them.

Exercise C

Look at the following newspaper reports. Find and write down:

1. three sentences about the past

2. three sentences about the future.

Police and coastguard stations were besieged with 999 calls after what were thought to be meteors were sighted off the Dorset and Devon coasts last night.

Dozens of people reported seeing bright white flares streak through the night sky just after 7 pm.

But there were no reports of any falling on land.

One flare was seen by the seven-strong crew of the Torbay lifeboat off Paignton as it returned from an incident.

A school in the West is to lead the way in a new campaign aimed at alerting children to the dangers of meningitis.

Pupils between 11 and 15 will be told about the brain disease and teachers will be encouraged to use a special pack of information in the classroom.

The campaign, by the National Meningitis Trust, will be launched at Backwell School in North Somerset tomorrow.

What happened when?

In stories, we do these things:
- we tell **what** happened
- we describe **when** it happened
- we explain the **order** in which things happened – what happened first, what happened next and so on.

Good writers make all these things clear by the words they use.

Exercise A

LISA has been reading about the history of hot air and gas balloons. Unfortunately her computer is having a bad day and has got all the sentences below in the wrong order. Work out the correct order and write the numbers of the sentences in that order.

The first balloons

1 Jacques Charles of France tried a gas balloon in 1783.
2 The hot air balloon rose four metres in the air, then threatened to set fire to the curtains!
3 Later that year, the Montgolfier brothers of France experimented with sending a duck, a sheep and a hen up in a balloon, before sending François Pilatre into the air.
4 The servants shot it down.
5 When it landed in a village the terrified French peasants hacked it to pieces.
6 In 1709 a priest showed a working model of a hot air balloon to the king of Portugal.

Exercise B

Read this report and work out exactly what happened and when. Then answer the questions. Answer each question using a complete sentence.

1 What should John have done first?
2 Did he?
3 Where did he go first?
4 What for?
5 What did he do next?
6 What happened?
7 Why was he saved?
8 When did other people know what had happened, and how did they know?

SAVED BY HIS STEPLADDERS

John's amazing lift plunge escape

An engineer cheated death when a pair of borrowed stepladders stopped a heavy lift as it hurtled three storeys down on to him.

John Coan was knocked off the steps as he worked in the lift well replacing cables. Amazingly, the half-ton lift jammed against the ladders three feet from the bottom, leaving 21-year-old John enough room to escape being crushed.

Last night he was comfortable in hospital with head, back and neck injuries.

John was working at a DSS office and had borrowed the aluminium steps from staff at the benefits agency.

As he cut the old cables the lift, which should have been secured, plummeted 30 feet.

Shocked office staff heard the crash, followed by a groan, and were sure John had been killed.

Diaries and plans

Many people use diaries to write down what they have done and their thoughts and feelings about their lives. We can also use diaries to write down things that haven't happened yet – plans and appointments. On this page we look at the diaries and plans of Engelbert Hunk, the well-known singer and TV celebrity.

THURSDAY

FRIDAY

Exercise A

Looking ahead

Engelbert Hunk's agent is briefing reporters about what the star will be doing next week. Use the information above to write five sentences describing the star's plans for Thursday and Friday.

Exercise B

Looking back

Engelbert keeps a diary in which he records the main things he does each day. Write his diary for either Thursday or Friday.

Time words

One of the ways we make clear when things happen is by using time words and phrases. Someone like **LISA** who is learning the language has to learn these. You already know a lot of them and use them without a second thought. For example:

- **past** *yesterday*
- **present** *right now*
- **future** *tomorrow afternoon.*

Exercise A

Help **LISA** by copying and completing the set of time words below. In each case the answer is a group of words – a phrase.

Looking back	Looking ahead
earlier today	later today
last week	
	in two days' time
a year ago	
	from now on

Exercise B

If **LISA** is going to learn how to use the phrases in Exercise A correctly, she needs sample sentences to show her how they should be used. For example:

Earlier today I lost my raincoat.

I shall go to the Lost Property Office later today to see if it has been found.

Write similar sentences for the other pairs of phrases, showing how they are used.

Lifelines

Where were you five years ago – and what were you like? Where will you be in five or ten years' time?

◄─────────────────────────────────────►

Five years ago   **Now**   **Five years in the future**

Looking at the past

A lot has happened to you in the last five years.
How much of it can you remember?

Exercise A

Make a chart like the one below and fill it in with as much information about yourself as you can. Start with 'now' and work backwards, because it's easier to remember things that way.

Year	Home	School	Important events in my life	Other important events I remember
1999	Baby Gemma born	Moved to Willingdon High School	Broke my ankle	
1998	Moved to Lodder			
1997			Won cup in swimming sports	Manchester won Premier League
1996				
1995				

Exercise B

Now you are going to write some sentences about your life over the past five years. *When you write them, you should start with the thing that happened first and move towards 'now'.*

❶ Pick out five things you want to write about.

❷ Think of a different way to start each sentence. Look at the word box on the right for ideas.

❸ Write your five sentences.

Word box

in 19--
a year later
the next year
after that
in the same year
by then
at about the same time
shortly afterwards

Looking into the future

You can't change the past ... but you can dream about the future! What would you like to be in your wildest dreams – in five years' time? In ten years' time?

Exercise C

④ Think of five dreams or ambitions for yourself.

⑤ For each one, think of a date when it will happen.

⑥ Write them down like this:

> 2005 Chosen to represent England in the Olympic Games 100 metres.

Exercise D

⑦ Now write a sentence describing each of your dreams or ambitions. Try to vary the time words you use, as you did in Exercise B on page 114. Use the word box there to give you some ideas.

Exercise E

⑧ Now look at all ten sentences you have written. Check that they make sense and that they say exactly what you want them to say. Cross things out and add to the sentences as you need.

⑨ Now write a final version of your sentences. Use these two headings:

- Looking at the past
- Looking into the future.

Summing up what you've learned

The past

Writing about the past can include:

- history books
- diaries
- newspaper reports describing things that have happened
- autobiography (writing about your own life).

The future

Writing about the future can include:

- weather forecasts
- horoscopes
- newspaper reports describing things that are planned
- personal plans.

Stories and reports

Stories and reports:

- tell **what** happened
- describe **when** it happened
- explain the **order** in which things happened – what happened first, what happened next and so on.

Sometimes events are not described in the order in which they happen. This is often true in newspaper reports, which usually put the most exciting or dramatic thing first and then explain how it happened later. The reader sometimes has to work out the order in which things happened.

Time words

One of the ways in which we make it clear when something happened (or when something will happen) is by using time words and phrases. For example:

earlier today	*later today*
last week	*next week*
two days ago	*in two days' time*
a year ago	*next year*
up to now	*from now on*
in 19--	*a year later*
the next year	*after that*
in the same year	*by then*
at about the same time	*shortly afterwards*

That's entertainment

LISA is finding out how people spend their leisure time at home. **LISA** wants to know:

- What is 'leisure'?
- Why do people spend so much time sitting in front of a TV set?
- What is football?
- Why do people watch it?

In this unit you will learn about:

Commentaries and reports
Reviews and blurbs
Verbs:
- the present tense and when we use it
- two different kinds of present tense.

Telling stories:
- in the past
- in the present.

How to write:
- about yourself
- a review.

Football

LISA has been getting interested in football. Her computer has collected the following three texts about the same match:

1

FIRST SPEAKER: Le Saux — comes forward — and that's Mark Hughes with the shot. Mark Hughes really caught hold of that. Schwarzer surviving a brilliantly hit shot by Mark Hughes.

SECOND SPEAKER: I mean that's vintage Hughes, isn't it? One touch in the box — with his least favourite foot as well —

FIRST SPEAKER: Merson towards Branca, but it's a bit long.

SECOND SPEAKER: — that's the first time that Le Saux had really ventured into the danger zone — quality ball in and an instant shot. Great save: great piece of football from both sides.

2

And it's Michael Duberry again, looking for Hughes — intercepted by Festa midway inside his own half. Fed to the far side to Kinder. Townsend has the ball now, over the halfway line down the Middlesbrough left. He hits it long, but Branca is offside and it's a free kick to Chelsea ... Good control by Hughes and passed there to Petrescu on the far side. Infield to Zola. Zola back to the halfway line.

3

Schwarzer was not beaten until two minutes before the hour, when Zola gathered a return pass from Dan Petrescu and drove the ball against the crossbar from 25 yards. By then Middlesbrough had seen what turned out to be their two best chances of winning fail to produce an actual shot.

In the 55th minute Merson found Ricard in space only for Sinclair to tackle the Colombian before he could bring the ball under control.

Exercise A

The three texts above are:
- ● a newspaper report
- ● a TV commentary written down
- ● a radio commentary written down.

1 Which is the newspaper report?

2 How do you know?

3 Which is the radio commentary?

4 How can you tell the radio commentary from the TV one?

Exercise B

Look again at the radio and TV commentaries above.

1 Make a list of the main differences between the kinds of information each one contains.

2 Explain why there are these differences.

That's entertainment

LISA is trying to make up her mind whether to read a book or watch TV …

Gaby Roslin makes dreams come true with *Whatever You Want* (BBC 1) but she is not exactly stretched.

Either people are easily pleased or she is working on a tight budget. Riding across Europe on a Harley Davidson, following in the footsteps of Julie Andrews in the *Sound Of Music* and meeting a ghost is not the stuff of my dreams.

But the contestants put such ambitions on a par with winning the lottery.

Three motorcycle couriers competed for an invitation to Harley Davidson's 95th anniversary celebrations by wheeling around on a mini-trike trying to remember who to deliver packets to.

A bearded biker called Scary Dave, who had a stud in his tongue, shed a tear when he won.

I hate to see a grown man cry, but Gaby thrives on that sort of thing. Any sign of emotion and she is beside herself with excitement.

2 'WANTED. Boy aged about twelve to star in a TV commercial. Excellent rates of pay. Must be boy-next-door type. Average looks. Acting ability essential.'

There are no two ways about it, Danny Thompson is a dead average kid: average hair, average nose, average eyes, and average freckles. But landing the starring role in a TV commercial turns out to be not quite as wonderful as it sounds!

In this hilarious sequel to *Dead Meat!*, we again meet Danny, his parents, his smelly baby sister, his mate Corky – and Pete, the singing dog, walks into Danny's life.

Exercise A
Read the two texts above and then answer the following questions about each one:

1 What kind of entertainment is it about?

2 What is the writer's purpose?

3 Why do people read this kind of writing?

Exercise B
Imagine that you are writing for the *Radio Times*. A new series called *Whatever You Want* is just starting. You have to tell viewers what it is about and why they will enjoy it. Write three or four sentences to go in the programme listings.

The present tense

LISA is learning more about verbs. This time her computer is being programmed to understand the present tense.

Exercise A

So far the computer has only got part of the present tense. The table on the right shows the parts it has understood so far.

Copy out the table and fill in the gaps.

	to walk	to be
I	walk	
you		are
he/she/it		
we	walk	
you		
they		are

Exercise B

Now **LISA** wants to know when we use the present tense. She has recorded four texts that use it in different ways. The verbs are all in the present tense and are all printed in **bold type**. Read the texts on the right and then write the answers to the following questions:

1 Imagine you are listening to text 1. When are the actions (*has*, *hits*, *is*) happening?

2 Read text 2. When do the actions (*do*, *visit*) happen?

3 Read text 3. When do the actions (*has*, *works*, *goes*) happen?

4 Read text 4. What kind of text is it? It is about a story that happened in the past. So why do you think it uses the present tense?

1 Townsend **has** the ball now, over the halfway line down the Middlesbrough left. He **hits** it long, but Branca **is** offside and it's a free kick to Chelsea.

2 On Tuesday I **do** the shopping and on Wednesdays I usually **visit** my Gran.

3 Dad **has** a delicatessen just down the road. He **works** there Monday to Friday and on Saturday mornings. Mum **goes** in to help him when she can.

4 In this hilarious sequel to *Dead Meat!*, we again **meet** Danny, his parents, his smelly baby sister, his mate Corky — and Pete, the singing dog, **walks** into Danny's life.

More about the present tense

I **AM SHUFFLING** THE CARDS

NOW I'M **DEALING** THEM OUT ON THE TABLE

LISA is a bit annoyed. She was just thinking she understood the present tense when somebody told her there are *two* present tenses!

Exercise A

Help **LISA** understand.

1 First of all copy the table below and fill in the blanks.

I	am walking
you	
he/she/it	
we	
you	
they	

We call the 'I walk' tense the **simple present** tense because it is simple – you haven't added anything to the verb. We call the 'I am walking' tense the **present continuous**.

2 Can you explain to **LISA** why we call it 'continuous'? Look at the pictures at the top of this page and see how the verbs are being used there.

Exercise B

LISA needs some more examples to feed into her computer. Look at the pictures below and write one sentence about each one. Use the present continuous tense in each sentence.

Now make up four more sentences of your own, using the same tense.

Talking about the present

Exercise A

The text that follows is about bees. It is describing things that are always true, so it is in the present tense. Some of the verbs are missing. They are listed in the verb box below, with some other verbs that don't come from the passage. Write down the number of each blank and the verb that you think should go in it.

Inside the beehive

Bees that __1__ together in nests are called 'social bees'. Well, you'd have to be social to live with *this* lot.

Quarrelling queens Usually there's just one queen in a hive. She __2__ her time laying eggs. But sometimes more than one queen __3__ out, and things can turn rather nasty. The first queen to appear __4__ off any rivals.

Drowsy drones It's a lovely life for a drone. Your worker sisters __5__ house for you. And they even __6__ you. You don't have a sting because you never __7__ to fight any one. There's just one problem. You've got to battle with hundreds of brothers for a chance to mate. If you mate with a queen you die.

Verb box

die	keep	need
feed	keeps	spend
feeds	kill	spends
hatch	kills	wants
hatches	live	work

Exercise B

The second part of the account is given below. In it, more verbs are missed out, but you have to work out for yourself what they should be. Write down the number of each blank and the verb that you think should go in it.

Bees make honey from the sweet nectar produced by flowers. It's horribly hard work. Some bees __8__ from 10,000 flowers a day. They often visit up to 64 million flowers to make just 1 kg of honey.

That's good news for the flowers because the busy bees also __9__ up pollen. They even have little leg baskets to carry it. The bee __10__ the pollen to another flower of the same type. There, some of the precious pollen brushes on to the flower, fertilises it and so __11__ it form a seed.

Why do you __12__ the flower goes to all the bother of making scents, bright colours and nectar? __13__ it all for us? No! It's to attract bees. Lots of bees means lots of flowers. See?

A bee __14__ her long tongue and a pump in her head to suck up nectar. She __15__ the nectar in a special stomach.

Past and present

Exercise A

Do you remember the book blurb on page 119? On the right here is the story of what happens when Danny goes for his TV audition. Stories are usually in the **past** tense. This one is unusual because it is all in the **present** tense. Read it and then answer the following questions:

1 This story could be written in the past tense. Look at the first two paragraphs. Most of the verbs are printed in **bold type**. Write the paragraphs out again, putting the verbs into the past tense. Like this:

> We **arrived** *at a big building in the middle of the city.* We **got** *a lift.*

2 Now look at the rest of the story and do the following things:
- write down each verb as it is
- write down the past tense form of the verb.

We **arrive** at a big building in the middle of the city. We **get** a lift to the seventeenth floor together with more scrubbed kids and their parents. I **look** around at the other boys. None of them **is** as average as me. I**'m** sure of that. We all **pile** out at the seventeenth floor. We **troop** along the corridor peering at each other. We **arrive** at the large office of the Sublime Advertising Agency.

The office **is** filled with lots of other kids and adults. Mum **says**, 'Now don't be disappointed, Danny. Regard all this as an experience in the trials of life.'

After a few minutes a man walks into the office. He goes up to various kids and mutters 'No' to them. Kids, looking as miserable as dead sardines, leave the office with their miserable parents. The man comes up to me.

'Hmm, maybe,' he says with a face as bland as a glass of milk. Then he moves on.

Exercise B

On the right is the beginning of a story in the past tense.

1 Write it out again, but use the present tense.

2 Write five more sentences continuing the story, still using the present tense.

Simon saw them come. The removal van lumbered down the road, followed by a red car, and both of them stopped at the end house. The children got out of the car and stood talking while their parents unlocked the house. Two boys and a girl.

The older boy was about Simon's age, and he looked disgusted. His voice floated up the road.

'This village is weird! There's no one about.'

Tell me about yourself

Hi, my name is Jay and I come from Wisconsin.

I live in a small town called Homeville. Tell me about yourself ...

When someone says, 'Tell me about yourself' it's sometimes difficult to know what to say. Here's your chance.

Exercise A: Collecting ideas

1. Make a list of things you can write about yourself. You could include:
   - **facts about yourself**
     name – age – appearance
   - **your home**
     what sort of house or flat you have – what your neighbourhood is like
   - **your family**
     what they are called – what they are like
   - **your school**
     its name – how big it is – your favourite subjects – your favourite teachers
   - **your interests**
     what you like doing in your spare time.

Exercise B: Sorting and planning

2. Look through your list and:
   - cross out the bits that look less interesting
   - circle the bits that are more interesting.

3. Rewrite your list. This time put the ideas in the best order so that they will make sense for the reader.

Exercise C: Writing

4. Now write seven or eight sentences about yourself. Write complete sentences. You should find that most of these use the **present tense**.

Writing a review

On page 119 you read a review of a TV programme. Now it's your chance to become a TV, film or book reviewer. Here's what to do:

1 Choose your subject

Choose one of these:
- a story book
- a feature film
- a TV drama, soap or other feature (one that tells a story).

2 Make some notes

Write a list of ideas about:
- the story
- its good points
- its bad points.

3 Write about the story

Now write four or five sentences explaining:
- who the story is about
- the situation – what is going on.

But don't give the ending away!

4 Write about your opinion

Now write four or five sentences describing the story's good and bad points. You might find it helpful to use some of the adjectives in the word bank below.

5 Finish it off

A good review finishes off with one or two sentences telling the reader what you thought about the story as a whole. For example:

Under the Weather is one of the most exciting stories I have read in a long time. If you like adventure stories about the sea, then it's definitely for you.

Write one or two sentences to finish the review off.

Word bank

action-packed	hilarious
comic	lively
complicated	moving
dull	sad
electrifying	slow
exciting	stodgy
fascinating	tedious
fast-moving	thrilling
flat	tragic
hair-raising	unfunny

Summing up what you've learned

Kinds of writing

Commentaries and reports

A **commentary** usually describes a piece of action – like a football match. It is usually spoken; the commentator describes things as soon as they happen. Commentaries usually use the **present tense**.

A **report** describes things after they happen. It uses the **past tense**.

Reviews and blurbs

A **review** describes a film, TV programme or book. It usually contains two kinds of information:

- what the book, film or TV programme was about
- the writer's opinion of how good it was.

A **blurb** is a short piece of writing which is meant to persuade us to buy a book or video, for example. It tells us a little about the story and then a lot about why it is so good! For example:

In this hilarious sequel to *Dead Meat!*, we again meet Danny, his parents, his smelly baby sister, his mate Corky – and Pete, the singing dog, walks into Danny's life.

The present tense

There are two forms of present tense in English:

	Simple present	Present continuous
I	walk	am walking
she	walks	is walking

The **simple present** is used for:

- repeated actions
  *She **walks** to school every day.*

- things that are always true
  *They **live** in Sunderland.*

- some commentaries
  *Zola **shoots!** – It's a goal!*

- some stories
  *So he **says** to me ...*

The **present continuous** is used for actions that are still going on. For example:

*The Queen **is talking** to the crowd.*

LISA becomes a reporter

LISA has decided that a good way to find out about life on earth is to 'shadow' a newspaper reporter.

The picture on this page shows the first story they cover. Look at it carefully. What do you think the story might be about?

In this unit you will learn about:

Reading and understanding newspaper reports

Verbs:

- the simple past tense
- the past continuous tense.

Writing sentences about the past

Writing a newspaper report

Can you believe it?

The story that follows is the first one **LISA** saw the reporter working on. Read it and then do the exercises below it.

A

BEST PALS Lawrence Henderson and David Mathias each reached into the far corners of their pockets to scrape together the 50 pence they needed to buy a refreshing drink from the school tuck machine.

Their thirsts were quenched as they shared the can on the campus of Crispin Community school in Street.

Then Lawrence noticed something different about the pull ring on the can, and to the 12-year-olds' delight they found it carried an £8,000 holiday prize for two.

They couldn't believe their luck and rushed home with their treasure, and Mrs Henderson confirmed it was a luxury holiday for two adults.

B

But the competition organisers are allowing each boy to take his family on a £4,000 trip, for, in the true tradition of their friendship, they are sharing their good fortune.

Lawrence's mother Jackie, of Wells Road, Glastonbury, who has another son Robert, said: 'It was a fantastic surprise.'

'We haven't got a clue where we are going yet. We have been too stunned to think about it properly.'

'It is the stuff dreams are made of. We have never been further than Cornwall or on a plane.'

'Everyone is coming up with suggestions for us, but we want to think long and hard about it first. Lawrence is looking for sun, sand, and watersports.'

Exercise A

1. The report above is divided into two main parts. Write one sentence explaining what the first part is about.

2. Write one sentence explaining what the second part is about.

3. Where it says 'A' there should be a headline and where it says 'B' there should be a smaller heading. What do you think they should say? Write them down.

Exercise B

4. The report above contains some words and phrases that are new to **LISA**. They are listed here. Write an explanation of what they mean:
   tuck machine   *campus*
   pull ring   *watersports*

5. The first paragraph ('Best pals ... machine.') is one long sentence. **LISA** finds it hard to understand. Rewrite it in two or three shorter, easier sentences.

Girls – playing football?

Below this is another story **LISA** saw the reporter working on.
Read it and then do the exercises that follow it.

Lucy the Lioness of soccer

If girls could play in the soccer premiership, then every top club in the land would have its scouts watching hotshot Lucy Bailey.

Diminutive Lucy, who is aged just 12, scored 48 goals this season in just nine games for the top London women's side Millwall.

Lucy from Trowbridge has been playing soccer for as long as she can remember after being introduced to the game by her stepfather Andy, who plays for local league side Bradford United.

Although Lucy can train with the boys at John of Gaunt school where she is in the first year she cannot play in their matches.

Her talents so impressed Paul King, who is the coach with Trowbridge Tigers, a boys' club she has trained with, that he gave her name to top London women's team – Millwall Lions.

After trials last year Millwall snatched up the Wiltshire prodigy, who can play 'anywhere up front'.

Currently Lucy – whose brothers Matthew, nine, and Tom, six, are also soccer-mad – plays every Sunday with the junior Millwall side, the Lionesses.

Manchester United fan Lucy's eyes light up when she talks about her team's success this season, in which she has played no small part. She said: 'We won one game 32-0.'

Exercise A

The report above doesn't tell the story in the order in which it happened. Read it again, and then answer the following questions:

1. Where did Lucy do her training at home? (2 answers)

2. Who told Millwall about her?

3. What team does she play for?

4. In what position does she play?

5. What is her goal average per match?

6. What is her team's highest-scoring match described in the story?

Exercise B

7. **LISA** finds the first paragraph of the report above difficult to understand – again!
Explain to her what it means by rewriting it in two or three easier sentences.

8. Would it be true to say that Lucy comes from a 'football family'? Give the reasons for your answer.

9. Explain the meanings of the following words to **LISA**:
premiership   *hotshot*
diminutive   *prodigy*

All in the past

The newspaper reports you have been reading use the past tense a lot. **LISA** has been collecting examples so that her computer can work out how we use the past tense and how it is formed. All the verbs in the following sentences are printed in red:

> Then Lawrence noticed something different about the pull ring on the can, and to the 12-year-olds' delight ... it carried an £8,000 holiday prize for two. They ... rushed home with their treasure, and Mrs Henderson confirmed it was a luxury holiday for two adults.

Exercise A

Help **LISA** understand how the past tense works by answering the following questions:

1. Write each of the verbs down on a new line.

2. Against each verb write the **simple present tense form**.

3. Write an explanation of how we form the past tense.

4. Write an explanation of when we use the past tense.

Exercise B

Not all English verbs follow the rules you explained in Exercise A. For example, we don't say, 'he goed', we say, 'he went'. Verbs that follow the rules are called **regular verbs**. Those that do not are **irregular**.

1. Some of the verbs in the list that follows are regular and some are irregular. Write down the irregular ones.

wave	hit	order
make	save	drink
find	comb	say

2. Write down the past tense form of each of the irregular verbs you have listed.

3. Write down the past tense form of each of these verbs:

hit	sing	cut
burst	hurt	

   Which is the odd one out and why?

I was thinking ...

You can't catch **LISA** out twice. She knows there are two present tenses. Now she has collected the following examples. Once again the **verbs** are in red:

> As I was going to school yesterday I saw Maria. I was walking along the high street and she was hurrying in the opposite direction. I shouted to her, but she just carried on towards the station. She was looking very worried.

*I don't suppose there are **two** past tenses, by any chance?*

The sentences above contain verbs in two tenses:

- the simple past
  I saw

- the past continuous
  I was going.

Exercise A

1 Copy and complete the following table of the past continuous tense:

I	was	going
you		
he/she/it		
we		
you		
they		

2 Look at the example sentences above that **LISA** collected. Write an explanation of when we use the simple past and when we use the past continuous.

Exercise B

1 **LISA** needs some more examples to feed into her computer. Look at the pictures at the bottom of this page and write one sentence about each one. Use the past continuous tense *or* the simple past tense in each sentence.

2 Now make up four more sentences of your own, using the same tenses.

3 Look back through your sentences. Underline all the verbs in the simple past. Circle all the verbs in the past continuous.

Trouble with a dog in a lift

The two extracts in the exercises below come from the beginning of a story.

THE LANGUAGE KIT 1

Exercise A

In the part of the story on the right, some of the verbs are in brackets. Write down the correct past tense form of each verb.

I'm glad there's only one more week of school before summer vacation. Today __1__ (be) so hot ! My clothes __2__ (stick) to me and my brain __3__ (feel) all tired out. I didn't even finish my maths in school. So now I have to do it for homework.

I __4__ (walk) into the lobby of my apartment building thinking how good a big, cold drink would taste. I __5__ (push) the Up elevator button and waited. When the elevator __6__ (get) to the lobby Henry opened the gate and I __7__ (step) in. Just as he was about to take me upstairs Peter Hatcher and his dumb old dog __8__ (come) tearing down the hall.

'Wait up, Henry!,' Peter called. 'Here I come.'

'Please don't wait, Henry,' I said. 'The elevator's too small for that dog.'

Exercise B

In the next part, shown on the right, some of the verbs are missing. They are listed below, but not always in the correct form or order (and not all the verbs in the list come from the passage). Write the number of each blank and the correct form of the verb to go in it.

Verbs

be   beat   believe
figure   have   walk
laugh   open   say
stink   strike
stuck   wonder

But Henry __9__ the gate and waited. 'This elevator can hold ten people or the equivalent,' Henry said. 'And I __10__ that dog is the equivalent of a person and a half. So with me and you and Peter and that dog we've still only got four and a half people.'

Sometimes I wish Henry didn't spend so much time thinking.

'Hi, Henry,' Peter __11__. 'Thanks for waiting.'

'Any time, Peter,' Henry told him.

'Excuse me, please,' I said, stepping out of the elevator. I held my nose. 'I can't ride up with that dog. He __12__!'

My heart __13__ so loud I was sure Henry and Peter could hear it. And I know Turtle, the dog, __14__ at me. He __15__ out his tongue and licked the corner of his mouth. I'll bet he could taste me already! I __16__ down the hall with my head held high, saying, 'P.U.'

Henry called, 'Ten flights up __17__ a long walk, Sheila.'

'I don't mind,' I called back.

132

Cheerless children

On this page you can read about what life was like for children in 'The Measly Middle Ages'.

Exercise A

In the following extract some of the verbs have been missed out. Read it through and work out what should go in each blank. All the verbs are in the simple past tense.

Parents __1__ little attention to children until they __2__ five or six. After all, they were probably going to die. Only one child in three __3__ to their first birthday. Only one in ten __4__ to their tenth. (No one __5__ birthday-cake candles in those days. There wasn't enough business!)

Parents in the Middle Ages may have been measly, but at least they __6__ a small improvement on Anglo-Saxon parents. Many of the Anglo-Saxons __7__ that a child born on a Friday would have a miserable life – so they __8__ them the unhappiness by killing them when they were born! Others 'tested' the new baby by putting it in a dangerous place – a roof-top or a tree branch. If it __9__ it was a wimp and was killed – if it laughed it __10__ .

Exercise B

In the section that follows, the verbs have been missed out again. Work out what should go in each blank. But this time the missing verbs are in different tenses – so be careful!

But life __11__ still very tough for children in the Middle Ages. If the plague didn't get you, then one of the other Middle Age marauders might! In 1322 Bernard de Irlaunde's daughter __12__ in her father's shop. A passing pig __13__ into the shop, __14__ the baby on the head and __15__ her. What a swine!

Children from rich families were cared for by nurses. The babies __16__ in tight bands of cloth so they couldn't move – this was supposed to make their legs grow straight. In fact the lack of use __17__ them weak for a year or two.

Neighbours!

LISA has asked you to help her with a news story she is reporting. The story is told in the pictures on the opposite page. Your job is:
- to work out what happened
- to write up the story.

Exercise A

1 Look at each picture carefully. Decide what it tells you.

2 For each picture write the number of the picture and then two or three sentences telling what happened.

Exercise B

Now think about verbs. In your sentences you have used a lot of verbs in the past tense.

3 For each picture look again at the sentences you wrote. Underline the verbs you used.

4 Look at the verb bank below. Find the picture number and see if there are any verbs you would like to use. If so, change your sentences to include them.

Exercise C

Now it's time to write your newspaper report.

5 Think of a good beginning for your story. It must make it clear what the story is about and it should be as interesting as you can make it.

6 Write your opening sentences. Then tell the rest of the story, using some of the sentences you wrote before and any new ones you think of.

Verb bank

1 live, reside, dwell, inhabit
2 park, arrive, visit, come, reach
3 lend, borrow, loan
4 cut, trim, lop, clip, prune, hack, slash, heap, pile, stack, throw, chuck, heave, pitch, toss
5 soak, drench, slosh
6 burn, blaze, roar, flare, flame
7 spray, soak, douse, flood
8 return, give back, reclaim, recover, ask, request, demand

9 throw, hurl, launch, fling, pitch, sling, toss, crack, shatter, break, fracture
10 shout, insult, curse, abuse
11 drag, tug, yank, jerk, pull, attack, assault
12 hit, strike, clout, whack, assault, attack, escape, struggle
13 enquire, question, interview

Summing up what you've learned

Verbs in the past

When we are telling a story or writing a report we are dealing with things that happened in the **past.** We can make this clear in two ways:

1 We can use words and phrases that tell the reader **when** things happened:
yesterday
a few years ago

2 We can put the verb into the past tense:
Yesterday I **was walking** along the road and I **met** Fiona.

The past tense has two different forms:

- the simple past
- the past continuous.

Forming the simple past tense

The simple past tense of **regular verbs** ends in **-ed**:

I save → *I saved*
I walk → *I walked*
I cry → *I cried*
I play → *I played*
I tap → *I tapped*

Some verbs are **irregular**. That means that they do not follow this rule. For example:

I run → *I ran*
I go → *I went*
I hit → *I hit*

Forming the past continuous tense

We make the past continuous tense of all verbs like this:

I save → *I was saving*
I walk → *I was walking*
I cry → *I was crying*
I play → *I was playing*
I tap → *I was tapping*

We use **was** or **were** followed by the **-ing** form of the verb. All verbs follow this rule.

Using the simple past and the past continuous tenses

We use the past continuous if we want to tell people that the thing we are describing went on for some time:

*She **was walking** slowly along the road.*

We use the simple past to show that the thing we are describing is completed, or has ended:

*I **caught** sight of Susan. She was walking slowly along the road.*

EXIT

TO PASS OUT
PULL HANDLE
AND LET GO.

Puzzling notices

LISA is finding English more difficult than she had expected. She thought we used things called sentences when we spoke to each other. Now she is finding that we sometimes don't use proper sentences at all.

- Look at the picture above. What does the notice in it mean?
- How would you turn the notice into a complete sentence?
- Can you think of other examples of notices that are not written in complete sentences?

In this unit you will learn about:

Newspaper headlines and other short messages

Complete and incomplete sentences

Verbs:
- what makes a whole verb.

Tables of information:
- how to expand information into complete sentences
- how to turn full sentences into tables.

How to make notes

In brief ...

LISA has collected all these spoken and written texts. But what are they, and what do they mean?

RETURN OF THE SOCCER THUGS

NO ENTRY

ONE WAY

Good morning!

12 years in jail for road rage maniac

Taxi! Taxi!

The Lost World: Jurassic Park

Exercise A

Two of the texts above are newspaper headlines. Pick them out and say what you think the newspaper report is about.

Exercise B

For each of the other texts above, write a short explanation of:
- where you might expect to see or hear it
- who it is meant for
- what it means.

Headline news

LISA would also like some help with English newspaper headlines. She just finds them confusing. Here are some she has collected:

Bike slimmer is nicked at 43 mph

£25,000 bill for a trip on a chip

TOP OF THE COPS!

Charity copter killed my birds

Explosive car park

Exercise A

For each of the headlines above:

1. Write down the headline.

2. Write a short explanation of what you think the newspaper story might be.

Exercise B

Now it's your turn to be a newspaper headline writer. Read both of the news reports below and then make up a headline for each of them.

A DIY dunce who wedged her finger inside a tap had to be rushed to hospital with the tap still jammed on.

The incident happened in Bath after the girl, in her 20s, tried to retrieve a washer.

Firefighters sawed through the tap but failed to release her and it was left to hospital staff to prise it off.

WILDLIFE campaigners are racing against time to save a wood that is home to one of Britain's rarest bats.

Cornwall Wildlife Trust needs to raise £6,000 quickly to outbid timber buyers at Prideaux Wood, St Blazey – one of the few breeding spots for the Greater Horseshoe Bat.

Is it a sentence?

As we saw earlier in the book, every statement sentence must have a subject and a verb. The people who wrote the 'sentences' below thought they were proper sentences, but they aren't:

1 *Walking through the park the other day enjoying the lovely summer sunshine.*
2 *The people next door but one to us in the big red house with the blue front door.*

Both 'sentences' leave us asking questions:

1 **Who** was walking through the park? The 'sentence' has no subject.
2 What did the people living next door but one **do**? The 'sentence' has no verb.

Exercise A

For each of the following sentences, write down:

    a the subject **b** the verb.

1 Some school subjects are really interesting.

2 Some can be seriously boring.

3 I really like science and maths.

4 My friend Katie absolutely hates French.

5 In science I like the experiments best.

6 Our science teacher Miss Gupta makes all her lessons interesting.

7 Geography and history can be fun, too.

8 Maths, on the other hand, is just hard work.

9 This week we are doing algebra.

10 All those x's and y's are so confusing!

Exercise B

Some of the following sentences are incomplete. For each sentence say:

    a if it is complete or not
    b if it is incomplete, what is missing.

1 I finished my homework early yesterday evening.

2 Decided to visit my friend Zoe.

3 A girl next door to the newspaper shop.

4 We've been friends for years.

5 Walking down her road.

6 Saw a strange light behind her house.

7 Bright blue colour and flashing on and off.

8 I got closer.

9 To see it more clearly.

10 It was just a police car parked by the newspaper shop.

The whole verb

When we say that a sentence must contain a verb, we mean a complete verb. As we have seen, the verb can take different forms and may be more than one word.

So far we have looked at the following tenses:

I was expecting you two hours ago!

	Simple present	Present continuous	Simple past	Past continuous
I	walk	am walking	walked	was walking
she	walks etc.	is walking	walked	was walking

These tenses are all from the verb **walk**. We have used three different parts of the verb:

- the **present tense** form
  walk or *walks*
- the **past tense** form
  walked
- the **present participle**
  walking

All these forms are made from the **stem** of the verb: **walk**.

Exercise A

LISA has to program her computer with the rules for making the tenses listed in the box above. She needs some help.

1 When we are making the continuous tenses of 'walk', what other verb do we need to use? Write down the forms of the verb that are used above.

2 Now explain how the present continuous tense is formed.

3 Now explain how the past continuous tense is formed.

Exercise B

LISA has forgotten that not all English verbs behave properly and obey the rules. Can you remind her how to make the **simple past tense** of these verbs:

go
choose
come
think
throw
run
stand
swim
say
catch

Expanding information

Information books often set out facts without using complete sentences.

Exercise A

The table below contains a number of facts about earthworms. We could write them out using complete sentences. For example:

Earthworms are found in most soils worldwide.

Write two more sentences using the facts in the table.

Name of creature:	Earthworm
Where found:	Most soils worldwide
Distinguishing features:	Segmented body. See-through skin. Slides along by squeezing its body segments forward.

Exercise B

The table below contains more information. Write four sentences using this information.

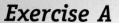

Antennae

Head

Centipede

Millipede

Name of creatures:	Centipedes and millipedes
Where found:	Worldwide, often amongst leaf litter and rotten wood
Distinguishing features:	Centipede: Segmented, slightly flattened body. Two jointed legs on each segment; two long feelers.
	Millipede: Segmented, rounded body. Four jointed legs on each segment; two short feelers.

Making tables

Exercise A

Use the information in the paragraph on the right to make a table like those on the previous page.

Romantic problems

Millipedes have a big problem – they can't see very well. So male millipedes have developed some strange ways of attracting a mate.

- Some bang their heads on the ground.
- Others let out a loud screech.
- Some produce special scents.
- Others rub their legs together to make sounds.

Exercise B

Now use some of the information below to make a similar table.

Feet count

Millipede means 'thousand feet' – which just goes to show that some scientists can't count. Millipedes never have more than 300 feet.

Centipede means 'hundred feet'. But once again the scientists got it horribly wrong! Many centipedes have fewer than 30 feet.

Walking

When a millipede walks, waves of movement pass up its body so that it glides along. When a centipede walks it raises alternate legs just as you normally do. It has extra long legs at the back so it doesn't trip up.

Millipede style of walking

Centipede style of walking

Jaws

Millipedes have munching jaws. Centipedes have poison fangs.

Making notes

When you are studying it is very useful to be able to make good notes. On this page and the next you can practise this important skill. Here is an example of note-making:

Butterflies and many moths have amazing coloured patterns on their wings. These colours are made up of tiny overlapping scales and they help male and female butterflies to find each other before mating.

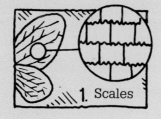

1. Scales

Butterflies and moths

amazing coloured patterns on wings

made of tiny overlapping scales

helps sexes recognize each other (mating)

How to make notes

1 Read the text carefully and make sure you understand it.

2 Work out what the important facts are.

3 Cut out all the unnecessary words. You don't want sentences, you want:

- single words (especially nouns, adjectives, verbs)
- short phrases.

4 Use colours to highlight important sections.

5 Use lines and arrows to show the links between things.

Exercise A

Make notes on the short text on the right. Follow the pattern of the notes above.

Butterflies can smell through their feet! That way they can land on a leaf and know what type it is. Which helps female butterflies to lay their eggs on leaves their caterpillars can happily eat.

3. Feet

SNIFF SNIFF SNIFF

14

Practice in making notes

Now use the same approach and make notes on each of the short paragraphs in the exercises below.

Exercise B

Butterflies and moths can detect smells using their antennae. The male Indian moon moth can scent a female over 5 km (3 miles) away. It follows the scent through woods – round trees and across streams – ignoring all other smells. That's like you sniffing your supper 75 km (47 miles) away!

Exercise C

Newly hatched *polyphemous* (polly-fee-mouse) moth caterpillars are tiny. But they start eating straight away and within 48 hours they increase their weight 80,000 times.
  That's bad news for the local greenery because the chomping caterpillars can strip all the leaves from a tree.

1 hour   24 hours   48 hours

Exercise D

The gruesome death's-head hawk moth has a sinister skull shape on its thorax. Its equally ugly caterpillars like to nibble the poisonous deadly-nightshade plant. The noxious nightshade makes the caterpillars taste so terrible that no one in their right mind would ever want to eat them.

thorax: its chest
noxious: poisonous

Exercise E

Brown-tail moth caterpillars are also pretty ugly. Their bodies are covered in sharp needle-like hairs that break off in your skin and make it itch like mad.

Is it a sentence?

We sometimes use 'sentences' that are not in fact complete sentences. A complete statement sentence must contain:

- a subject
- a complete verb.

Statement sentences often also contain other parts as well.

Brief messages

Sometimes we deliberately use incomplete sentences.
Examples are:

- notices
- some newspaper headlines
- some titles of books, films and TV programmes.

Unfinished sentences

At other times we write sentences that are just incomplete. We forget to put in a subject or a verb.
Examples are:

- *Walking down her road.*
- *To see it more clearly.*

A complete verb

We have seen that verbs can have different **tenses.** Some tenses are just one word:

	Simple present	**Simple past**
I	walk	walked
she	walks	walked

Other tenses are more than one word:

	Present continous	**Past continuous**
I	am walking	was walking
they	are walking	were walking

Parts of the verb

Verbs have these parts:

Stem	walk	go
Present tense	walk/walks	go/goes
Past tense	walked	went
Present participle	walking	going

Making tenses

We make the present continuous tense by adding am/is/are to the present participle:

I am walking   they are going

We make the past continuous tense by adding was/were to the present participle:

I was walking   they were going

Making notes

1. Read the text carefully and make sure you understand it.

2. Work out what the important facts are.

3. Cut out all the unnecessary words.

4. You don't need sentences, you need:
   - single words (especially nouns, adjectives, verbs)
   - short phrases.

5. Highlight important sections.

6. Use lines and arrows to show the links between things.

LISA gets ready to go home

LISA's year on earth is nearly over. Soon she will travel back to her own planet.

- ○ What do you think she will remember most about her stay on earth?
- ○ What do you think she will be most happy to get away from?

In this unit you will revise:

The what, who, why, where and how of language

Subjects and verbs

Time and tense

Present tenses

Past tenses

Writing reports

Looking at language

We can work out a lot about the things we read and write by asking five simple questions:

What?

We talk and write about many different subjects during a day. There are special words for different subjects.

Who?

We write and talk differently for different people.

Where?

For example: is it spoken or written? Is it a book, a magazine or a newspaper?

How?

The four main kinds of writing people do are:

- stories
- descriptions
- explanations
- opinions and arguments.

Why?

We write and talk for many different purposes and this shows in the words and sentences we use. Here are some common purposes:

- to inform
- to instruct
- to persuade
- to entertain
- to interact (to get on with people). Examples of this are letters to people and telephone conversations with friends and relations.

Exercise A

After each of the following four texts there are three of the five questions above. Answer each of them as fully as you can.

Running down stairs harms dogs, vet warns

Dogs that bound up and down stairs and sleep on their owners' beds run the risk of becoming deranged and lame, vets have warned.

a Where? **b** Why? **c** What?

We've got new cars to show but nothing to hide.

At Daewoo, we have a reputation for doing things differently. And once again we've lived up to it, by launching three brand new car ranges at once: the Lanos, the Nubira and the Leganza. But although our cars have changed, our transparent pricing policy remains the same, so you still won't find any hidden extras.

a Who? **b** What? **c** Why?

3

Using the emulsion brush, apply the wash to the wood, working always in the direction of the grain – you should be able to see it through the thin wash. Allow to dry a little (15–20 minutes).

a What?   **b** How?   **c** Who?

4

It was raining lightly on May 14th 1962, and spring showers are always welcome in the Great Plains. Farmer Emil Ziebart of Ethan, a town in south-eastern Dakota, glanced at the churning clouds massing in the south-west. He decided that there was just time to plough another furrow before supper. Nearing the end of the round, he checked the sky again. A greyish-black cloud wall about half a mile wide loomed over his neighbour's tree grove. Below it hung a funnel-shaped mass, tapering towards the earth. Then suddenly, as he stared, horrified, the trees disappeared, flicked up as easily as a vacuum cleaner sucks up dust specks.

a What?   **b** Where?   **c** How?

Exercise B

For each of the following newspaper headlines, write one or two sentences saying what you think the news report is about.

1 FA rejects German shirts for England

2 Rare whales threatened by Japanese salt works

3 The boy of five sent 50 miles on a train alone

4 Death row pet wins his appeal

5 PC Piglet joins cops

Exercise C

1 When you read a horoscope you expect to find sentences about the future. Where else might you find them?

2 What tense would you use to write a story?

3 If you were giving a commentary on a sports match what tense would you use?

4 Which of these words and phrases might you use in an argument?

*afterwards   because
therefore   during
proof   soon*

Subjects and verbs

Exercise A

LISA has been checking how well her computer understands the parts of a sentence. Help her by correcting the printout below.

    a Write the number of each sentence.

    b If the computer has put the right subject and verb, put a tick against the number.

    c If it has made a mistake, put a cross and write the correct answer.

1 The bruised Brits had been battered for a thousand years.

    Subject: The bruised Brits
    Verb: had been battered

2 It will become mild and windy in the south.

    Subject: It
    Verb: will

3 You'll hear from an old friend.

    Subject: You'll
    Verb: hear

4 The car crashed.

    Subject: car
    Verb: crashed

5 He spotted a long tail hanging from the bottom of his car.

    Subject: He
    Verb: spotted a long tail

6 I'm going to get even with her.

    Subject: I
    Verb: 'm going

7 You are at your friskiest today.

    Subject: You
    Verb: are at

8 On 28 September he died in battle.

    Subject: On 28 September he
    Verb: died

9 This is not a day to be shy.

    Subject: This
    Verb: is not

10 In 1066 the Normans finally nobbled them.

    Subject: the Normans
    Verb: nobbled

Exercise B

It's clear that **LISA** is still getting things wrong. Help her by writing two short explanations:

1 what the subject is and how to spot it

2 what the verb is and how to spot it.

Time and tense

Exercise A

Each of the sentences below describes something in:

- the past, or
- the present, or
- the future.

Decide which is which. Then write down the number of the sentence and whether it describes something that is past, present or future.

1. We visited Chichester yesterday.
2. I live in London.
3. I will give you your pen back tomorrow.
4. School is going to be closed for the whole of next week.
5. That car is out of control.
6. She is having a holiday in New York next month.
7. You cannot be serious.
8. I was only joking!
9. So he goes up to this bloke and asks him the time.
10. Water freezes at 0° Celsius.

Exercise B

The verbs in the sentences below are either in the present tense or in the past tense. Decide which is which. Then write down the number of the sentence, the verb, and whether it is in the past or present tense.

1. She saw her uncle yesterday.
2. He gave her a birthday present.
3. They always go to Benidorm for their holidays.
4. Bennie hates hamburgers.
5. The ref was gobsmacked.
6. Peter is mad about model planes.
7. Mary needs help at school.
8. The team plays away next Saturday.
9. Dan never reads story books.
10. There was a loud bang.

Exercise C

1. Write one or two sentences explaining what we mean when we say that a sentence is in the past.

2. Write one or two sentences explaining what we mean when we say that a sentence is in the present.

3. Write down the simple present tense of 'walk'.

4. Write down the simple past tense of 'walk'.

Present tenses

Exercise A

LISA has been reading about insects, but her computer has recorded the information wrongly. Find the mistake in each of the sentences below. Write down the word that is wrong and against it write what it should be.

1. Giant stick insects looks like ugly old sticks.

2. And they grows to a whopping 33 cm (13 inches) long.

3. The Queen Alexandra's birdwing butterfly from New Guinea boast a wingspan of 38 cm (11 inches).

4. But that're nothing – a mere 300 million years ago there were giant dragonflies with wingspans of 75 cm (30 inches)!

5. Cute little fairy flies am actually tiny wasps only 0.21 mm long.

6. The good news are, they don't sting humans.

7. There are a species of Australian dragonfly that can reach 58 km (36 miles) per hour.

8. Aphid females gives birth to live young.

Exercise B

Each of the sentences below also contains a mistake. Find them and write them down in the same way as in Exercise A.

1. Everyone is knowing about ants.

2. They're easy enough to identify in the summer when they are marching into your home to inspect your kitchen.

3. Ants can be pretty awful – they are getting everywhere from your plants to your pants – but they can be awesome, too, in all sorts of horrible ways.

4. Honeypot ants are squeezing sticky honeydew from aphids.

5. They are doing the aphids a favour, they are not needing the sickly stuff.

6. The ants are keeping feeding this honeydew to particular ants in their nest to make them swell up like little beads.

7. The swollen ants are then sicking up the honeydew to feed the rest of the nest. Awful!

Exercise C

1. Look at the mistakes in Exercise A. They were all made because the computer did not understand one rule. Work out which rule it is and then write an explanation of it.

2. Now do the same for Exercise B.

15

Past tenses

Exercise A

You are an editor. The story below is written in the present tense. Usually stories are told in the past tense. Rewrite this one in the past tense.

When I come home from school that day Mum is in the kitchen. She has a big wok on the stove and she's busy dicing vegetables and meat on her chopping board.

Bub Tub is sitting on the kitchen floor looking for bits of dust to eat. Who needs a broom when Bub Tub is around?

'Ayo, Anny.'

'G'day Bub Tub. Hi, Mum.'

I help myself to whatever looks good in the fridge, tell Mum about my day at school, and go to my bedroom. I sit at my desk and think about my homework. I find yesterday's gum stuck to the underneath of my desk, unstick it and put it in my mouth. I stare out of the window. I stare at my poster. I chew. I remember Mr King's threat. He will have a word or two with my parents if I don't shape up with my homework. I pull out my exercise book and do some maths.

Exercise B

In the following story, some of the verbs have been missed out. They are listed at the end. Write the number of each blank and the verb that should go in it. Make sure that you write the correct tense of the verb you have chosen.

Once upon a time an old Carib woman __1__ with her people on the bright clean land of the moon.

They __2__ a happy people and the dark-haired moon children __3__ nothing better than jumping up in the air and trying to catch the floating moonbeams.

One day, however, the old woman, whose name was Baba, __4__ tired of gazing out on the moonlight and __5__ her little home.

She __6__ no idea of where she was going.

She simply walked and walked and walked until, without even realizing it, she __7__ to the edge of the moon.

The old woman nearly __8__ over.

'Oh my!,' she __9__, pulling herself back just in time.

She __10__ there, at the edge of the moon, peering down below her.

Verbs

be	have
come	leave
fall	like
gasp	live
get	stand

LISA has 'fun'

LISA has has been trying out some of the entertainments people on earth enjoy. She has written a short report on each one and has asked you to check her English. As you can see, she has made a number of mistakes.

Exercise A

In the report that follows, **LISA** has got all the forms of the verbs wrong.

1. Find each of the verbs.
2. Write down the number of the line each verb comes from.
3. Write down the form of the verb **LISA** has used.
4. Write down what it should be.
5. **LISA** hasn't given her report a title. Make up a suitable title.

A group of children from Class 7R take me to a strange kind of entertainment. It be at a place they call a 'Community Centre and Youth Club'. They pay some money to a person at the entrance. Then we go inside. We go into a large room. There be no light coming in
5 from outside. Instead of the lights they uses in their school classrooms, there be coloured lights. These move around the room. There be a very loud noise. My computer measure it. It be too loud to being safe for human beings! The noise have a strange throbbing rhythm. It come from some machinery on a stage at one end of the
10 room. This be controlled by a human. Sometimes when the noise stop he shout at the people in the room. His voice be made louder by the machine. The room be full of people. While the noise go on they move around the room in a strange way. It not be like ordinary walking. Instead they jiggle around in time with the throbbing sound. The
15 sounds and lights be bad for my computer, so after a while I leave the room. I stand outside the hall. It be raining.

Exercise B

In the following report, **LISA** has mixed up some of the parts of some of the sentences. Find the sentences that are wrong and write them out correctly. When you have finished give the report a name.

The Green family invited me to stay with them for a weekend. On Saturday the country said we were going into Mr Green. We went in the family car and travelled for about an hour and a half. Mr Green stopped the car in a wide open space full of cars. We out got. On the back of the Greens' car were fixed some strange machines. Mr Green unfixed them and each member of the family took one. Two wheels had each machine. The wheels were wider than those of a car, but thinner. They were joined together by metal tubes. A small seat had to sit on you at one end and hold a bar at the other. Then you your feet on two things called 'pedals' put. By turning these around you could make the machine go along. Into some woods travelled we. The track was very muddy and bumpy. It was difficult to stay upright on the machine. I did not understand why it enjoyed they.

Exercise C

The report on the right is incomplete. **LISA** wrote it in note form and forgot to write it out in full. Write it out for her in complete sentences. Then give it a title.

England – have – time called 'summer'
very important
say   'We'll be able to do that in the summer.'
         'I can't wait for the summer holidays.'
summer – months – June, July + August
not as cold as – 'winter' – rains a lot
rain – very bad for – computer + electrical connections
'summer' – different sports from – winter
stop – football – play – 'cricket'
very difficult – understand
lasts – longer than football
players wear white clothes – stand around in – big field
do nothing most of – time
three in – middle – move around
one has – small round object – throws at – one – holding
– piece of wood
this one tries to strike it with – wood
if – successful – players all run around
'games' of 'cricket' can last – five days
often – rains – players allowed to go home.

LISA tries to understand

Exercise A

You have seen the problems that **LISA** has in understanding what human beings get up to in their spare time. In the pictures above, you can see four more spare-time activities. Choose one of them and think about what **LISA** might make of it. She has never seen this activity before and has to describe it for creatures on her planet who have never seen it at all! Write her report using correct English sentences.

It is time for **LISA** to return to Planet K48Z46. All her friends from school are offering her presents to take back with her.

The problem is that there is very little room in her spacecraft. She can only take five things with her.

How should she decide what to take? Perhaps you can help her. She wants things that will help her explain what life is like on earth – things that will remind her of her visit here.

What to do

1. Make a list of things that **LISA** might take. List as many as you can think of.

2. Against each one write a few words saying why it would tell creatures on her planet what life is like on earth or remind **LISA** of her stay.

3. Choose the best five.

4. Write one or two sentences about each one, explaining what it is and why you have chosen it. You could use some of the sentence starters below.

Sentence starters

- I would choose ... because ...
- Another thing that would be good is ...
- One of the best souvenirs for **LISA** would be ...
- I also think **LISA** should take ...

Memories

LISA has met a lot of people and done a lot of things since coming to earth. What do you think are the strongest memories she will take home with her?

Choosing the memories

In this book we have seen some of the things that **LISA** has done during her visit on earth. But of course she has done a lot of other things too.

1. Make a list of things that **LISA** might have done during the year:
   - places she might have visited
   - people she might have met
   - things she might have done.

2. Now choose two of these to think about in more detail. Choose two that are interesting to write about and that are very different from each other.

Writing LISA's story

LISA is writing an account of her memories. She is describing each memory as a little story. Her English is very good now, but she still finds earth people very strange.

Write her account of her two memories:
   - Tell the story of what happened
   - Describe **LISA's** thoughts and feelings about it.

LISA's departure

At last the time has come for **LISA** to go back to her planet. Write two short descriptions of what happened:

A diary account

You are one of **LISA's** friends. You have known her since she arrived on earth nearly a year ago.

You have watched **LISA's** departure. Now write up your diary for the day. Describe:

- what happened
- your thoughts and feelings.

A newspaper report

You are the reporter from the local newspaper. You met **LISA** in **Unit Thirteen**. Now you have watched her depart for Planet K48Z46. Write your front-page report:

1. Begin with a short but exciting description of the take-off.

2. Explain who **LISA** was and where she came from.

3. Describe some of the things she has done while on earth.

4. Say how the children and teachers at the school feel about her departure. (You could put in some short quotations of things they have said.)

Acknowledgements

With special thanks to Llantarnam School, Torfaen, Royal Manor School, Portland and Monks' Dyke School, Louth, for commenting on and trialling material.

The author and publisher would like to thank the following for permission to reproduce copyright material:

David Kitchen for material on pp20, 21, 24, from Llantarnam School; Reed Books for use of extracts from *The Trial of Anna Cotman* and *The Monster Garden* by Vivien Alcock, published by Methuen Children's Books 1989 and 1988, pp28, 30, 29, 32; David Higham Associates for extracts from *The Wonderful World of Henry Sugar* by Roald Dahl, published by Cape 1977, p28; *The Mirror* for the reproduction of extracts from the following articles: 'Sari mother rescues kids', 'Blonde women just aren't fair', 'Want a new look? Hair's how', 'Bear necessity', Russell Grant – Taurus horoscope (6/3/98), 'Saved by his step ladders' (6/3/98), 'Weekend view' (30/10/98), 'They had to faucet off' (6/10/97) 'Batty about conservation' (6/10/98), and for the use of the following headlines: 'Bike slimmer is knicked at 45mph' (17/10/97), 'Charity copter killed my birds' (17/10/97), 'Don't mark homework' (6/2/98), pp38–9, 40, 109, 111, 119, 139; extracts from articles with the following titles have been printed courtesy of the *Western Daily Press*: 'Sue halts peacock rampage', '20 mile ride in runaway juggernaut', 'Teenagers get phone box blues', 'Beach team goes on patrol', 'West is hit by meteor storm', 'Brain bug facts go to pupils', 'Jackpot joy in a can', 'Lucy the Lioness of soccer', pp38, 42, 88, 99,109–110, 128–9; *The Express* for extracts from articles entitled 'One in 100 suffers the killer allergy' (5/2/98), 'Exploiting the Princes' pain' and 'Princes in look-alike film fury', by Ian Gallagher (6/2/98), pp38–9; Solo Syndication for extracts reproduced from articles entitled: 'Finny facts' (*Daily Mail*, 6/2/98), 'BMW purrs 1500 miles with a cat in its bonnet' (*Daily Mail*, 6/3/98), the headline 'Boy of five sent 50 miles on a train alone' (*Daily Mail*, 3/4/98) pp39, 108, 149; *The Independent* for use of extract from an article entitled 'Instructor talks down man on crisis flight' (1/4/92), p42; *The Guardian* for use of extracts from articles entitled: '20 killed as jet slices cable car wires' by John Hooper (4/2/98), 'The plane that flew solo' by Martin Kettle (25/11/98), 'Robson suffers new heartache in extra time' by David Lacey (30/3/98), pp43, 54; Proton Cars (UK) Ltd for advert on p55; Sheil Land Associates Ltd for extracts from *Kitchen Blues* by Rabbi Lionel Blue, copyright © Lionel Blue 1985, published by Victor Gollancz, pp58, 61; the illustrations and text reproduced from THE USBORNE BOOK OF SCIENCE EXPERIMENTS by kind permission of Usborne Publishing, Usborne House, 83–85 Saffron Hill, London EC1N 8RT. Copyright © 1990 Usborne Publishing Ltd, pp62–5; thanks to Severn Trent Water for use of the extract from *Lake Vyrnwy*, published by Severn Trent Water, pp68, 74; Wayland Publishers Ltd for extract from *Britain Today: Farming* by Ray Woodcock, published by Wayland Publishers Ltd 1995, p68; extract from *The Shrewsbury Quest* reprinted by kind permission of The Shrewsbury Quest Ltd, p72; Kelloggs Management Services (Europe) Ltd for reproduction of the front and information from the back of *Kellogg's Frosties* pack, p79; use of text © Martin Oliver, 1988, first published by Scholastic Ltd, in *Groovy Movies* by Martin Oliver from the 1996 edition, p81; Heinemann Educational Books for use of extract from *Stepping Up* by Jane Liddiard and Molly Hemens, published by Heinemann Educational Books, p89; Random House UK Ltd for extracts from *The Eighteenth Emergency*, by Betsy Byars, published by The Bodley Head 1974, p92; Scholastic Ltd for the extracts from *Blood, Bones and Body Bits*. Text © Nick Arnold, *The Measly Middle Ages*. Text © Terry Deary, *Ugly Bugs*. Text © Nick Arnold and Illustration © Tony De Saulles, 1996, all published by Scholastic Ltd 1996, pp102, 99, 108, 122, 133, 142–5, 152; extract from *Truly Terrible Tales: Inventors*, by Terry Deary, reproduced by permission of Hodder and Stoughton Limited © Terry Deary, pp103, 111; David Higham Associates for the extract from *The Castle Diaries 1964–70* by Barbara Castle, published by Macmillan, p108; BBC Worldwide Ltd for use of extract from commentary to football match broadcast 29/3/98 at 3pm, pp118–20; ITV for the extract from the commentary of *The Big Match*, televised 29/3/98; © *The Guardian* for extract 3 on p118 by David Lacey; Scholastic Australia for extracts from *Dead Average* by Moya Simmons, pp119, 120, 123, 126, 153; the extract from *The Demon Headmaster Strikes Again* by Gillian Cross (published by OUP, 1996) on p123 is reproduced by permission of Oxford University Press; Random House UK Ltd for the extract from *Otherwise known as Sheila the Great* by Judy Blume, published by Bodley Head 1979, p132; Ewan MacNaughton Associates for 'Running down stairs harms dogs, vet warns' by Roger Todd and Catherine Elsworth (*The Sunday Telegraph* 19/4/98), the headlines 'FA rejects German shirts for England', ' Rare whales threatened by Japanese salt works', pp148–9; Duckworth Finn Grub Waters for reproduction of the text taken from a Daewoo advertisement published in *Sunday Telegraph Magazine* (19/4/98); *Country Living Paint Recipe Book* by Liz Wagstaff (Quadrille Publishing Limited) for use of the extract on p149.

The publishers have made every effort to trace the copyright holders, but if they have inadvertently overlooked any, they will be pleased to make the necessary arrangements at the first opportunity.

The publishers would also like to thank the following for permission to reproduce photographs on the pages noted:

Wayland Publishers Ltd, p68; John Seely, p69; Getty Images, p73; Pictor International, p73.